THE HOUSE AND CRAFTS BOOK

THE HOUSE AND CRAFTS BOOK

Over 100 Ideas in Full Color

compiled by Annelike Hoogewegen
        Hummy Eijlders-van der Tonnekreek
        Noortje de Roy
        Thea Wamelink

translated by Patricia Crampton

The Dial Press
New York 1974

The Dial Press
1 Dag Hammarskjold Plaza
New York, New York 10017

© copyright 1971 *Uw Huis vol Ideeën,* Meijer Pers b.v., Amsterdam

The original material for the text of this book was conceived by
Fogtdals Bogforlag a/s. Copenhagen. Illustrations on pages 58 and 59 are
from Spectator Publications, Stanley Works (GB); page 66 from
IMS-Copenhagen; pages 81 and 83 from Margerite Walfridson, Sweden;
pages 122 to 126 from ABC Press–'Elle'.

Text of this edition © copyright
Angus and Robertson (UK) Ltd, 1974

ISBN 0-8037-3786-6
Library of Congress   73-17945
Printed in Great Britain by Colour Reproductions, Billericay

Believe in your house

Not so much 'do it yourself', more 'express yourself'–this is the idea behind *The House and Crafts Book*. Believe in your home, for after all, it is more than the necessary packaging to protect you against wind and weather. Give the collection of 'little boxes' in which a great part of your life is spent an atmosphere which makes living in them a continuing experience. And even if the first great step is generally left to the builder, this simply prepares the living area for the atmosphere of warmth, comfort, companionability, creativity which you yourself must bring to it–even if you have two or more left hands.

The House and Crafts Book is not a book which says you have to do things. It is rather a collection of ideas about how to do things, mostly so simple that you can easily tackle them yourself. Moreover, the ideas have been selected in such a way that they offer unlimited possibilities for variation. We have also included a fascinating section on creative activities for you to do with children, or for them to do themselves. Throughout we emphasize the importance of your personal touch. That personal accent gives every home the atmosphere which suits its occupants.

Contents

A welcome on the mat

To new visitors the entrance or hall is a house's visiting card. Although the entrance is frequently cramped for space, so many everyday activities take place here. This is especially true in a flat, where the front door is the only entrance and exit. It is worthwhile counting up how many times you pass through the hall in one day.

Children have to be helped into their coats, only to come back from school later in the day to put down their satchels, take off wet boots, find a space for caps and mittens. Before a party, the hall is the place where you welcome guests, and hang up their coats.

So the hall must have a welcoming atmosphere. The first impression can be very important to new visitors. Here you can play with colours to your heart's content. Because the wall areas are usually small, and since you will not be spending hours on end in the hall, you may use striking colours. It is really a matter of finding the right colour combinations. Light, vivid colours make a space seem larger. If there are any angles or awkward lines, blur the incongruities with wallpaper in a small, adaptable pattern. In old houses with high ceilings a narrow passageway is particularly forbidding. The ceiling can be made to look lower by painting it in a dark colour or lining it with dark wood. Choose a low-hanging light, shining downwards, so that the ceiling is left in darkness. The lowering effect can be further accentuated by hanging photographs or prints on the walls in frames which are wider than they are high.

If you are renting your house or flat remember to choose a light which you can take with you when you move. In a small entrance, fixed or built-in cupboards are preferable. For example, a glove box attached to the wall is better than a storage cupboard on legs. A good compromise between moveable and built-in furniture can be provided by box units from a storage system which will accomodate a variety of things—coats, shoes, umbrellas, etc.—in individual sections.

By giving the cupboards sliding, folding or concertina doors, you can save considerable space. But you can do without doors, too—halls or passages already have enough of these.

An open cupboard, yes, and a really well-organised whole. The coats are out of sight as you come in, though the side wall is made up of free-standing rods. There are coat hooks at toddler height and a drawer for each member of the family. Use the space overhead as fully as possible, for instance with upper cupboards as shown here.

9

Upstairs and downstairs

Not many people possess 'staircase wit', yet the look of the stairs and their immediate surroundings can usually be improved. We go up and down stairs many times a day, and there is always a section of wall which meets the eye, ascending or descending. Turn this section into an eyecatcher. Paint or paper the wall black, for instance, and decorate it with prints, photos, appliqued dried flowers, a knotted rug, a relief, old weapons or a wall-hanging. Remember to use non-reflecting glass over prints, for direct lighting can cause an annoying reflection on ordinary glass.

Some houses may have rather difficult, space consuming stairs. The area under an awkward, steep staircase like this one can be augmented with an open or closed storage space. The underside of such a ground floor staircase is an ideal place for a slant-sided set of shelves to provide space for shoes, boots, shoe-cleaning materials, and so on. The shelf heights can be adapted to the height of what you want to stand on them.

A stout rope, knotted under the existing stair-rail, offers a helping hand to small stair climbers.

A board over the bottom steps represents a surmountable obstacle to toddlers. Adults generally step straight over it.

The niche of an unused or disused door is all too frequently regarded as a useless space. Yet it can be put to very practical use, as shown here, by fitting shelves and a mirror.

Because grown-ups' rails for coat hangers are useless to small children, help the little ones out by attaching to the wall a fold-back fixture made with a swivel arm. Buy some small clothes hangers for them to use with the new wall fixture.

An ugly staircase can be made more attractive to the eye; for instance by painting the steps in light colours or removing the bannisters on the passage side; this gives a more open effect. If there are small children in the house, linoleum or fixed carpeting is safer on the stairs than a runner. Worn treads must be levelled off and built up at the front with PVC profiles made specially for this purpose. Plastic profiles are also available for finishing off steps after you have put down linoleum or carpet. These can be stuck on with a special plastic cement.

Playing with colours

This section is not meant as a recipe for perfect colour combinations
—simply as a guide towards learning to use colours within the colour
ring at the bottom of page 15.

The ring consists of six colours, three primary colours and three derived
from them. The primary colours are red, yellow and blue. From them
are derived: purple (red + blue), green (blue + yellow) and orange
(red + yellow). To create a particular atmosphere in a room you must
choose an appropriate colour pattern. A warm sunny note is struck with
yellow, orange and red tones predominating, as in the picture on page
14. If you want to create a lively, effervescent impression, you should
use colours mainly from the blue-red sector. In order to accentuate
the effect, use strong colours. If you take the same colours, but lightened
—mixed with white—the result will be less striking, more on the gentle
side.

A cool, fresh interior is assembled from colours in the blue-green range
(page 12). And here too, strong shades emphasize the effect. By mixing
with white, you tone the colours down. Colours in the yellow-green
field create a calm, passive atmosphere and are very suitable in rooms
intended for rest and relaxation.

Obviously the possibilities of expression in colour are limitless: they can
be used to create a particular atmosphere and project a personality.

All colours within a quarter-circle, defined by two primary colours, will
—because they are related—harmonize with each other. You can use a
range of shades from one quarter-circle, or take just two colours, for
instance, as a point of departure. You can then use these two in various
nuances, toned down by white or darkened with black. There is no real
objection to expanding the relationship over a semi-circle. But in this
semi-circle you must then adopt only one basic colour, from the centre
of the semi-circle. All the shades on either side of it will then contain
something of the basic colour.

As a rule you should use pale, toned-down colours for the large surfaces
and the striking shades for small articles.

Combining related colours is not the only possibility. You can also work with the colours on opposite parts of the ring, that is, contrasting or complementary colours. To do this you must first decide which is to be the principal colour. If you want to give equal standing to two contrasting colours, it might be better to reduce one of the two basic colours by mixing with white. Otherwise the colour areas will compete with each other.

An effective colour-scheme can also be achieved by taking two or three related colours as the principal ones and adding one contrasting colour, partly in order to stress the main colour and partly to create a certain tension. This type of composition is obviously never dull. On the other hand, the shade-on-shade method is very popular. You pick one colour, in a wide variety of shades. As a rule of thumb, you can assume that one colour should be bright, another very pale and a third dark. After that you can play with a large number of intermediate tones.

To end this colourful tale, a word about grey. Grey is a colour, too. The neutral shades, from white through grey to black, are extremely suitable for creating an interplay between light and dark. The neutral colours can be used in any colour composition.

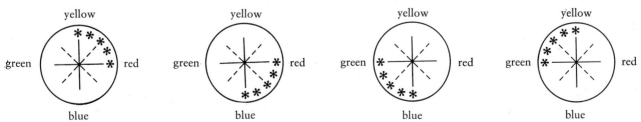

The personal touch

Atmosphere is an intangible concept. Purely tangible objects are the basis of house decoration: furniture, curtains, wall coverings and a carpet, for instance. The arrangement of all the tangible objects and the combination of colours reveal a person's taste. And sometimes taste helps to create an atmosphere in which everyone feels good—sometimes because there are no sharply defined rules about atmosphere. Ornaments are extremely important in the decoration of a room: paintings, works of art, a vase of flowers, an antique clock in a very modern room, theatrical posters, old sign-boards. Anything you admire and display will give the room a personal touch.

An ornament may be an heirloom, or something discovered by chance in an attic, or in a little shop. But unless the selection and placing are carefully thought out, the chosen piece may detract from the overall effect of your room: then the balance will be upset. Like furniture, ornaments must be regarded as useful objects. Never hang just any picture in an empty space on a random hook. A fine work of art often may not fit in with the whole and should—however much it breaks your heart—be removed.

There are countless objects and countless ways of displaying them— really more than can be fitted into the average house. Avoid the traditional and discover how the inside of your house can become an extension of your personality. Whether what you choose or buy is art with a capital A is not really important.

In the illustration opposite, there are a number of familiar kinds of wall decorations. But the variety and the arrangement are unusual, and tell you a lot about the character of the person who chose them. It must be somebody with lively and varied interests. If the rest of the house is equally as unorthodox and filled with objects—each one with its own personal value—then the resulting effect—in defiance of all traditional rules—will be right.

What appeals to you and what suits the room? These two factors must always be considered.

That door is closed

Removing an unused door usually involves knocking out the door frame and carefully filling up the opening. In an old house the demolition may cause cracks in the plaster and in a rented house it won't be allowed at all.

So why not leave the door where it is, and use the space for a striking wall decoration? It may be practical to remove the handle before hiding the door behind a beautifully decorated hardboard panel.

Buy a piece of hardboard $\frac{1}{2}$ in. (1 cm.) smaller in length and width than the inside measurement of the door frame. This means you will have $\frac{1}{4}$ in. (4 mm.) left on all sides—just enough to enable you to put the decorative panel in place and later, on, if you wish, to remove it.

Of course you know those landscape wallpapers covered with a woodland scene, castles, Venetian canals, etc. They are ideal for a panel like this. An enlarged photograph is another possibility. Or use scissors and paste and every possible type of paper to design a mosaic. You can really use anything for this, from ordinary wrapping paper to gold and silver foil.

The panel opposite is made of hardboard painted black, decorated with applied motifs mostly made from matt coloured paper—only the three flowers at the top were cut from glossy paper, for variation. You may copy each colour-section of the pattern—by tracing half of each shape on folded paper and cutting it out.

But why follow this design slavishly? Give your own imagination a chance.

It is fun to play with self-adhesive plastic, which can be bought in any colour, in gold and silver, and in countless different designs. First cut the pattern exactly to measure and then remove the protective backing. Unusual colour effects can also be achieved with self-adhesive felt. For instance, make a geometrical pattern using six shades of green.

To fasten the hardboard onto the door drill two holes in the top left- and right-hand corners of the board, about $\frac{1}{2}$ in. (12 mm.) across and 1 in. (2.5 cm.) from the top. Fix two long, round-headed screws—2 in. (4–5 cm.) long—in the corresponding positions on the door. The heads should be smaller than the holes in the panel. How far these are screwed in depends on the number of boards you want to hang on them.

There's music in it

In the top of this rectangular box there is a loudspeaker; under it, at a right angle, is the TV set (back shown here), then under that the record-player, radio, and records. (If you have no separate loudspeaker, you can put anything else you wish in the space above the TV set.)

This box cupboard can stand almost any-where, or if you add (concealed) castors underneath, you can move it about. Why not store the telephone and directories in such a box? Magazines and news-papers?

In the cupboard above you can store a radio, TV set, record-player, loudspeaker(s) and gramophone records. The frame is made of 1 in. (22 mm.) chipboard, back and shelves of $\frac{3}{4}$ in. (19 mm.) chipboard. Priming and painting chipboard is a difficult and time-consuming job. So, if you can, choose chipboard which has already received its first layer of finish—usually a transparent polyester primer. Then finish off

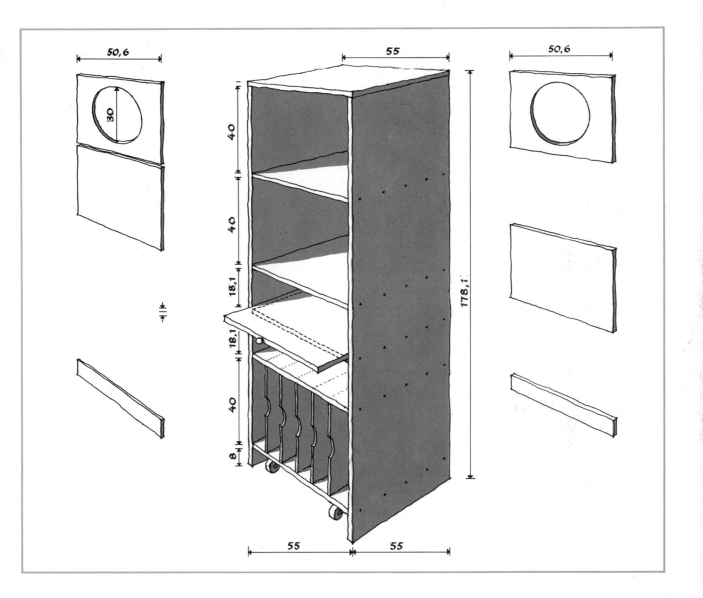

the chipboard with a coat of paint. Or choose double-sided plastic chipboard, and finish off the edges with plastic strips.

The sides of the cupboard can be held together with adhesive and/or screws (pre-drill holes). Make the vertical divisions in the record-holder from $\frac{1}{4}$ in. (4 mm.) hardboard; glue them into position and, if necessary, secure them with panel pins.

A bit of floor on the wall

This coat-rack wall is handsome both in colour and design. The wall has been covered with purple linoleum; the round white enamelled bars with their hanging hooks create a contrast as area dividers. The toddlers' reach has been taken into consideration. The backless white boxes complete the job.

A colourful and practical finish for walls is a special covering called dadolene. It is a thin backed plastic sheeting obtainable in widths of 54 in. and 45 in. (137 cm. and 144 cm.) and in many different colours. Cutting the strips to measure is not difficult with a special linoleum knife, but the supplier will usually do it for you.

A rough wall surface must first be smoothed: or you can cover it by nailing sheets of hardboard to it. The nails must be countersunk and the holes filled in. There are special types of adhesive available for fixing linoleum—you can generally get them when you buy the material—and you can also use hardboard with adhesive on one side. Newly plastered walls must be both smooth and properly dried. If the plaster is old, check that it is sound and remove loose flakes. Repair cracks and holes with a filler. Thoroughly wash painted walls and doors with water and detergent, and allow them to dry. After applying the adhesive, unroll and hold the linoleum firmly against the walls, cut away the projecting edges and then fix into place with the help of a hand-roller, which you might be able to borrow.

If you are fairly dexterous with scissors and paste and want to express yourself in a cheerful wall or door decoration, make these stars, wreaths and hearts.

Stars, wreaths and hearts

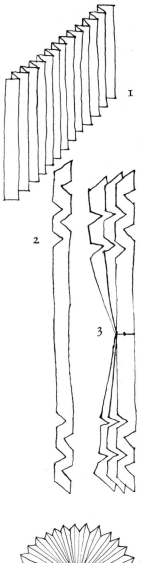

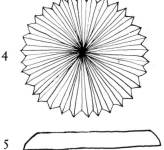

The silver star with the gold centre consists of four different stars glued together. The largest is made of silver paper 10 × 22½ in. (25 × 55 cm.) folded in a concertina pleat 1 in. (2.5 cm.) deep. (fig. 1). Cut the corners off diagonally and snip V's along the edges (fig. 2). Tie a wire round the middle (fig. 3) and place dots of glue between the pleats on either side of it. When the glue is dry, open up the star. The second star is made of flowered wrapping paper 8 × 19½ in. (20 × 50 cm.). Make it as you made the silver one, but round off the corners as in fig. 5. The third star, made of silver paper, measures 5 × 17½ in. (13 × 45 cm.) and its pleats are ¾ in. (1.5 cm.) deep. Leave these ends straight. Make the gold centre out of orange lining or wrapping paper 4 × 12 in. (10 × 30 cm.), pleats ½ in. (1 cm.). Clip the ends diagonally.

Glue the four stars together in the middle. Then glue the back of the largest star to a piece of cardboard, diameter approximately 10 in. (25 cm.), and use the cardboard for attaching the star to a door or wall.

The rosette with the white centre is made in almost the same way as the silver star. Except for the white centre piece, do not cut the ends of the concertinas. Use lining or wrapping paper for the coloured sections and drawing paper for the white centre. Dark blue: 12 × 60 in. (31 × 150 cm.), pleats ¾ in. (1.5 cm.). Lighter blue: 9½ × 27½ in, (24 × 70 cm.), pleats ⅞ in. (2 cm.). Red: 7½ × 17½ in. (19 × 45 cm.), pleats ¾ in. (1.5 cm.). White: 4½ × 6 in. (11 × 15 cm.), pleats ¾ in. (1.5 cm.).

The gold wreath is made from double-sided gold paper foil, six sheets 4½ × 19½ in. (11 × 50 cm.). Fold the sheets in two lengthwise, and clip the open long edges into fringes ¼–½ in. (½–1 cm.) in width. Cut to within ⅞ in. (2 cm.) of the fold. Make a ring of one strip of fringe and glue the ends firmly together. Stick the other strips to it one by one. The folded edges must all lie on the same side. Glue a ring of wire to the back of the wreath. Then curl the fringes in and out so that the wreath is nice and thick.

The heart with roses is mounted on a frame of chicken-wire 3½ × 24½ in. (9 × 62 cm.). Roll the wire lengthwise into a cylinder and bend it into a circle. Then shape it into a heart. For each rose you will need a piece of crêpe paper 2¾ × 13½ in. (7 × 35 cm.). Fold the strips of paper lengthwise, and stick a piece of tape to a corner on the inside. Paste along the open edge of the folded paper and roll up the strip to make a rose. Fix the roses to the chicken-wire with tape. Then cover any visible chicken-wire with green tissue paper cut in 2¾ × 6 in. (7 × 15 cm.) strips. Fold them widthwise and push the strips, closed edge down, into the chicken-wire. Stick the leaves together on the under-side.

It ought to be framed

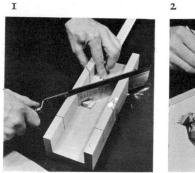

1

2

3

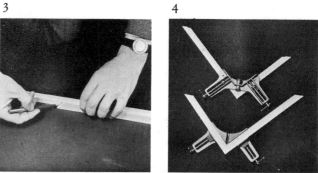

4

Having a frame made for anything you want to hang up is generally a very expensive matter. However, if you've tried framing something yourself, you may have discovered that this apparently simple job caused you more headaches than you expected. Yet anyone who has not too many left hands can do it, if he or she only knows the tricks. If you are making a frame for the first time, it is best to begin with a completely flat face. The corner

joints of frames are mitred—at an angle of 45°— with the help of a mitre block (1).
Place the picture against the ridge of a piece of frame (2) and mark the exact measurement on the top of the wood, preferably leaving a margin of 1/8 in. (2 mm.). Then place the piece of wood in the mitre block and adjust it so that the saw crosses the wood exactly on the marked spot. Hold the wood firmly while you saw. Saw another, similar, length, also mitred; mark off and saw the short sides (3).

5

6

7

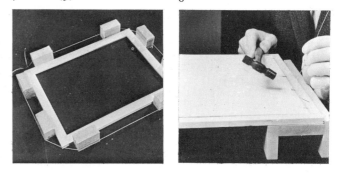

8

The four sides can be assembled in different ways. With the first method you use special frame clamps (4) which first clip the sides together two by two. Make sure that the sides match exactly, so that the ridge will be underneath the picture on all four sides when you have assembled them.
For the second framing method take strong thin string and eight wooden blocks to hold the frame. All the mitred corners of the frame are glued and

then fitted together by hand. First, place one block in the middle against each side of the frame as it lies on the table—with newspaper underneath. Tie the string round them and twist it into a loop. Push the blocks towards the corners (5). Then insert the other blocks in the positions shown (6) between string and frame. Finally move all eight blocks close enough to the corners (7) to prevent the string from touching the frame. According to the instructions on the jar or tube of adhesive, remove any which has squeezed out of the joints. After about four hours cut the string. After the adhesive has dried and the string cut, reverse the frame and place it on two supports. Use the mitre box on one end, for instance (8), and two of the small blocks you've used on the other. Place the polished glass inside the ridge, then the picture, and finally a piece of cardboard cut to size. Secure this with small tacks pushed into the frame. You can also make the cardboard a little larger than the picture, so that it fits over the back of the frame. Fix it to the frame with a stapler or some tape.

Another framing method: four pictures mounted on paper or board, stuck behind glass and then hung on the wall as a quartet. Use braid or velvet ribbon to suspend each picture. Use a textile adhesive to glue together the pieces of ribbon between the pictures. Thus, the openings in the hanging ribbons should be tight enough to cling firmly to the pictures when they are inserted. The brass rings at top and bottom, attached to the ribbon, hold the decoration firmly against the wall.

Set in gold

When attics are being cleared out, old picture-frames sometimes come to light and are often thrown away. But not so fast! Why not gild them and hang something unusual inside them? The examples opposite speak for themselves.

If you want to gild the frame, scrape off the existing layer of paint, scrub the frame, fill in any cracks and prime it. Then paint on gold paint—mixed with a little ochre. Gold shoe cream gives a beautiful effect as a finishing coat, applied with a sable-hair brush.

If the frame is particularly handsome, you could even cover it with gold leaf, which is obtainable in 'leaflets' 3 × 3 in. (8 × 8 cm.). You will also need a special liquid (gold size), a gold brush—made of squirrel hair—and, sometimes, a burnisher.

To frame projecting objects like veteran cars, it is best to make a showcase, as explained below.

Paint the outer side and ridged edge of the frame with gold paint and ochre.

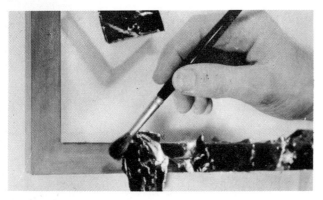

Apply the gold leaf with a good brush and a special gold burnisher.

Finally, wipe with a wad of cotton wool.

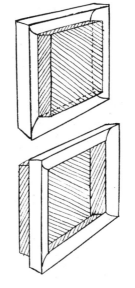

The showcase on this page can be placed in and on the frame. The sides—6 in. (15 cm.) deep—and the back are made of three-ply or hardboard. Glue and tack the parts together. For strength, nail or glue small crossbars behind the corners—remember which side will be visible. Cover the right side with rust-coloured, green or black felt. Then glue the box to the back or front of the frame, using a good adhesive.

29

Brightening up the ceiling

You can still find decorative plaster-work on the ceilings of old houses. Why not make an attractive eye-catcher of a big surface like this by introducing some colour into it. First the old surface must be cleaned with detergent and plenty of constantly changed clean water.

An especially stylish and decorative note is struck by this simple plaster rosette. Colours are the important element here.

After the surface is thoroughly dry, paint the large area of the ceiling with a soft shade of washable paint. Take small quantities of this basic paint and mix in other colours to make up the various shades for the rosettes, which must be more striking. Paint the ceiling with a large brush or roller and the rosettes with a long-haired brush—not too large.

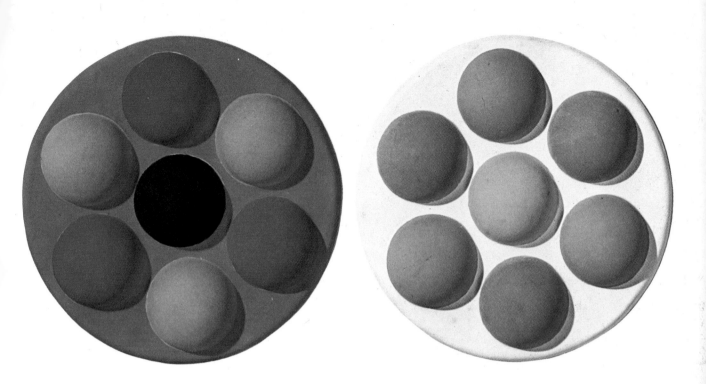

The secret of making successful plaster lies in adding the plaster to the water, not *vice versa*. If there is still a layer of water lying on top of the plaster poured into the mould, leave it there. It will be absorbed automatically into the plaster.

An old, dull and flat-surfaced plaster ceiling can easily be made more attractive by attaching plaster moulds bought from the plasterer and painted beforehand to your liking. These decorations are better made of polyester, but then of course they must be treated with a special plastic paint which adheres to polyester. You can also make plaster moulds yourself, for instance, by moulding them in a baking tray. Be sure to rub the cups in the baking tray with green soap so that the plaster mixture does not stick. Use ordinary plaster or a special 'hobby' plaster, sold in hardware and do-it-yourself shops. Mix plaster and water in an old basin, shaking the mixture—better than stirring—until the air bubbles have vanished and it has become a slow-flowing porridge. Pour the plaster into the cups and, to get the best results, remove it only when it is really hard. The length of time to harden depends on the type of plaster used. Remove the plaster moulds from their wells and let them dry, round side up, for a day. Then they can be painted and cemented to the ceiling.

A lamp to your taste

This detailed mosaic was made from pieces of foil of different colours. It represents many hours of creative work.

These days you see them everywhere—those extremely simple hemispherical lampshades in opaque glass or polyester. The latter is a favourite material with designers and hobbyists for all sorts of purposes. Both glass and polyester can be painted with acrylic paint or heat-resistant plastic paint. With such a hemisphere to work on, you can design a unique lampshade for yourself and your friends.

Some colours give a completely different effect when light shines through them, so before making a definite choice of colour, test them in advance, using an extra piece of polyester to see if your design will still be successful when held in front of a light source.

34

Be inspired—but not dominated—by these examples. Be your own designer and your lampshade will be truly original.

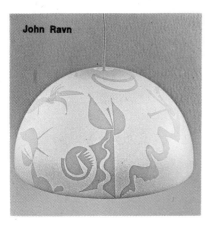

John Ravn

Poul Gernes

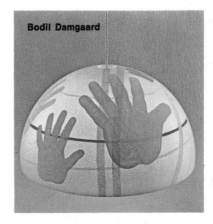

Bodil Damgaard

Poul Gernes

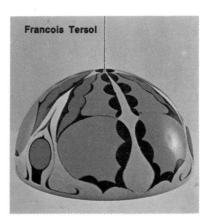

Francois Tersol

Søren Birk Pedersen

Lasse Wied

Poul Agger

Jørgen Haagen

35

Coloured peep-holes

In wintertime, you can brighten up window panes with decorations that give a flavour of stained glass. Hang them in front of the window so that daylight produces colourful effects.

The basis of these mobile peep-holes is twelve white or coloured strips of card ¾ in. (1.5 cm.) wide. The length of the strips depends on the size of your window. In the frames using white thread or nylon fishing line (which is all but invisible) suspend shapes which can be made of gold or silver foil, transparent paper, drinking straws or painted, light-weight polystyrene globes.

To make the frame, start in the top left-hand corner. Stick the corners of the top horizontal bar and the left-hand vertical bar together. To make sure of an accurate 90° corner, check it with a T-square.

Stick the vertical strips over and under the horizontals by turns, to achieve a woven effect. Keep checking to make sure that all corners are perfectly square, because the frame must be geometric.

When you have finished the frame and the mobiles, fix them to the frame with thread or nylon attached to the frame with sticky tape, preferably on the side of the card which is out of sight. If you want to hang the mobile peep-shows in the middle of the room, make a double card frame.

A variation can be introduced into the design of peep-holes by varying the size of one or two of the squares, or by surrounding an extra-large central square with a border of matching squares. A very free variant is the central illustration below: a sun made of gold foil with decorative peep-holes has been hung inside the circle cut in a piece of red card.

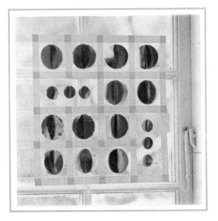

Gold flashers

Decorative birds can also be used to brighten up a window, or made into a mobile. Use gold foil, thin transparent plastic (sandwich bags), beads and sequins. The 'golden rain' is made of circles of foil stuck together in pairs on a thread.

Make the birds like this: trace the two patterns on transparent paper and cut them out. Cut out the top pattern once in transparent plastic and the lower one twice—mirror-wise—in gold foil. Stick the gold patterns on either side of the plastic one. Decorate the birds with beads and sequins or etch a design on the gold foil with a knitting needle. By making the raindrops the size of a coin and impressing a coin relief on the front and back you can thread together a chain of golden coins. If you give free rein to your imagination there are, of course, lots of other possibilities.

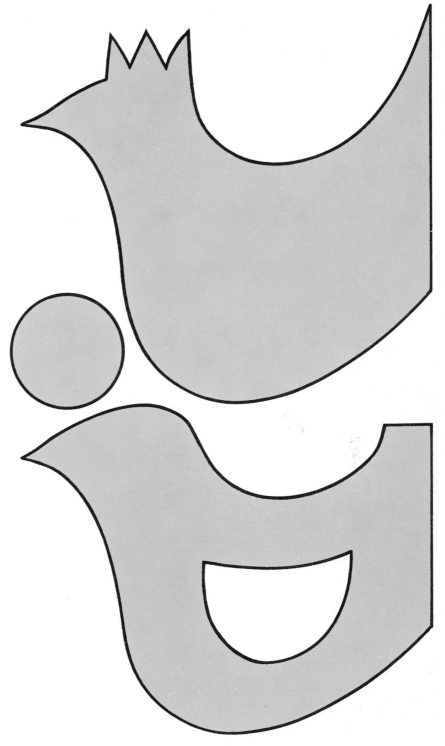

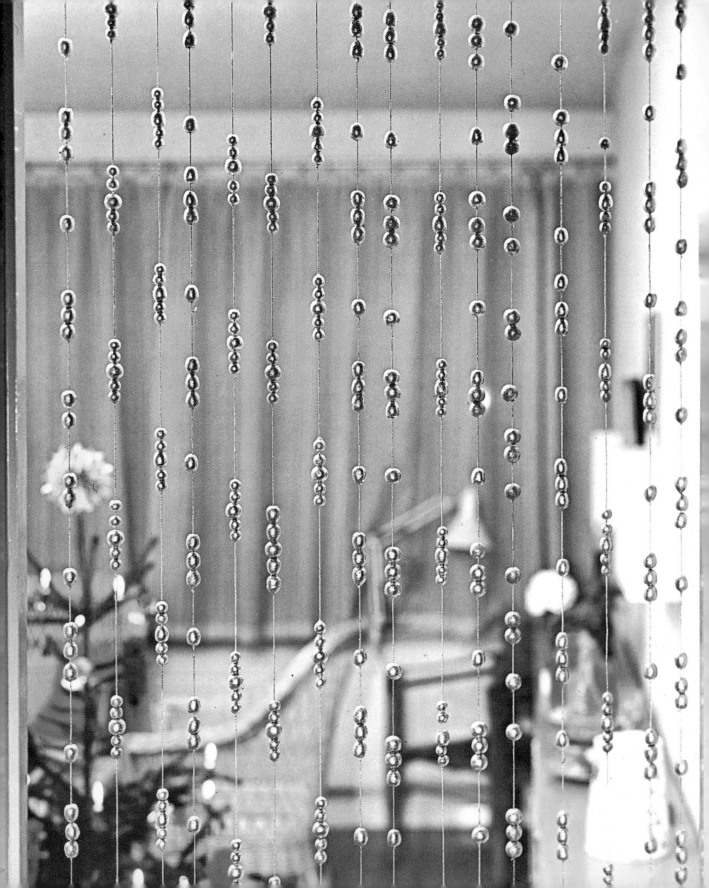

The bead curtain (left) is made of cotton-wool balls dipped in gold-bronze paint and strung on gold wire when dry.

The plaque (above right) is an oval piece of chipboard covered with gold foil. Nails dipped in gold paint serve as hangers for the glass bubbles hung on golden thread.

Wood mosaic. Wood can also be used to make simple and attractive articles to enliven an interior. This mosaic consists of fragments of carpenter's waste (from broomsticks, frames, etc.) glued to a background of an appropriate colour—for instance a remnant of wall panel or a piece of varnished chipboard.

The all-purpose box

Bar, tool-box, pick-up and record-holder, newspaper rack, toy-box—
by adapting the model shown here, these are just a few ways in which
this box can be used.
The construction is extremely simple. To make the sides, bottom and
lid, use ½ in. (12 mm.) chipboard. Make sure that two sides are 1 in.
(24 mm.) shorter—i.e. 22½ in. (57.6 cm.)—than the other two, so that

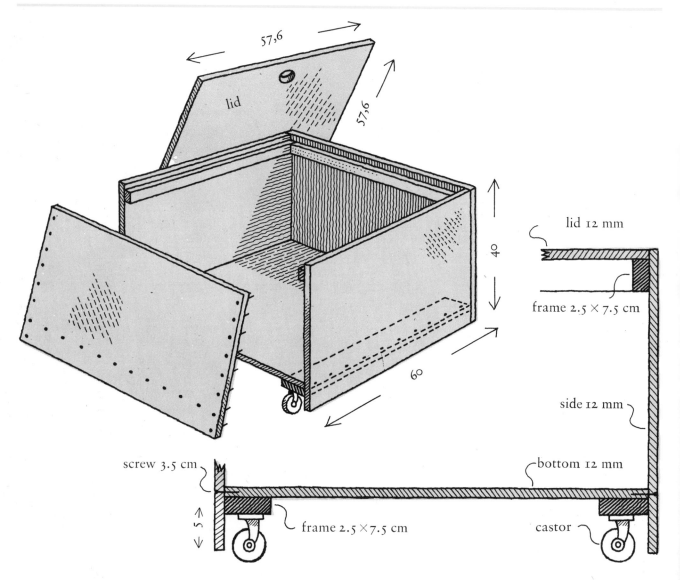

you will have a completely square box. Put the sides together with glue and/or 1½ in. (3.5 cm.) screws (pre-drill holes). Attach the bottom so that the castors project about ¾ in. (2 cm.) below the side panels. Remember to make a finger-hole in the lid or attach a handle to it. All variations of this design are also made of ½ in. (12 mm.) chipboard, including the compartments and dividers.

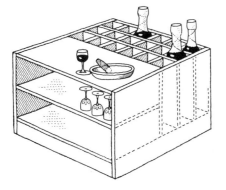

1. As a bar the box provides space for glasses and bottles. When working out compartment sizes, remember to allow for large bottles.

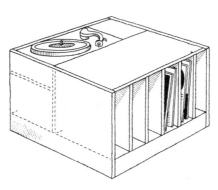

2. In this variation. allow enough space for the records to stand upright.

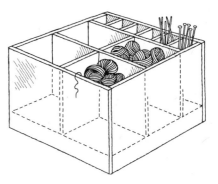

3. Adapted to the requirements of enthusiastic knitters, this design has large compartments for wool and narrow ones for knitting needles. It can also be adapted to other handicrafts.

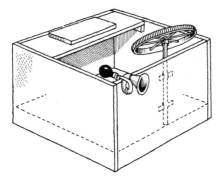

4. Every toddler wants a car of his own. If you haven't an old steering wheel and don't know where to get one, you can buy one in plastic complete with assembly kit, and with a horn as well.

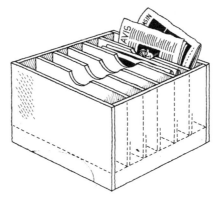

5. Create order out of newspaper and magazine chaos. This box can also take records, but preferably standing on its side, to prevent dust accumulating on the records.

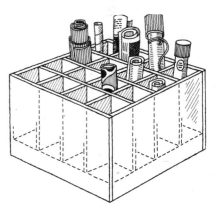

6. For drawing materials and oddments you can adapt the design to whatever you want to keep in it. It is not necessary for all the compartments to be the same size.

These beach pebbles have been painted with poster-paint and finished off with two coats of transparent varnish. Some stones have shapes which suggest a particular idea—for instance an animal's head. Take advantage of these natural shapes.

44

Beachcombings

Collections of stones and shells—mementos of a lovely holiday—can be made into attractive wall decorations and paper-weights. On a piece of white enamelled chipboard, make a fish out of shells glued into position. It is also possible to set the design in the paint while still wet. In this case apply the paint very thickly and press your shell pattern into it. To make the design illustrated below, frame a piece of chipboard with a slightly projecting frame. Paint the board with a very thick layer of white cement mixed with sand. Use one part sand and two parts white cement, add water, and stir constantly until you have a nice mash. Then spread an even layer of this on the board with a priming knife and press the shells into it. Plaster can also be used to fix the shells, but it hardens quickly and you will have to work fast.

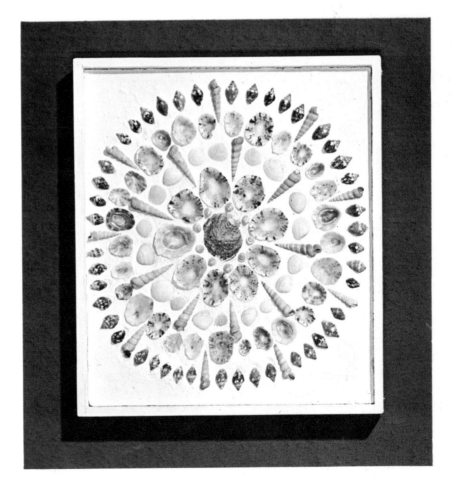

Start with the all-purpose box shape described on pages 42–3; use the same materials to make objects to save time and space.

For instance, sometimes drying the wash can present problems. On showery days bringing it in and taking it out again takes up a lot of the housewife's time. Every house needs a drying place which is not an eyesore. This homemade clothes-horse, in which the washing is only visible from one direction and which serves as an extra table in kitchen or bathroom, is an excellent solution. You can fix it to the wall or leave it to be moved from one room to another.

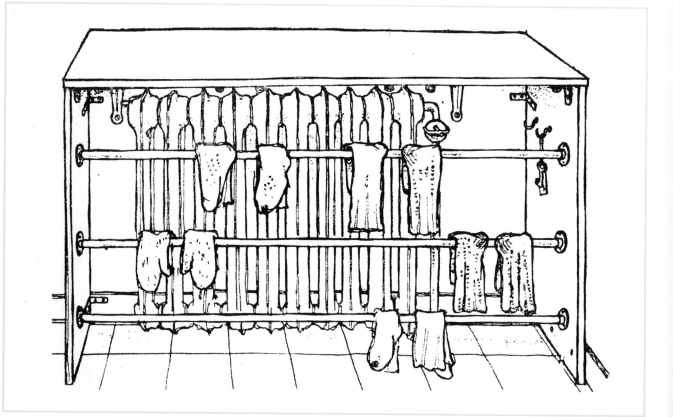

Anyone who likes to refer to her recipe book while she is cooking will benefit enormously from a 'lectern' attached to the wall above the work surface. This sort of stand can be put together in a twinkling, out of three oddments of block or chipboard.

It is even easier to make a handy kitchen knife-holder. All you need is a medium or largish cigar-box as shown in the sketch. Suspend the box from hooks screwed into the wall, having first attached small loop-screws to the box.

Where shall we put the ironing-board? Here are two examples of ironing cupboards where both the board and the clothes to be ironed can be kept. In the left-hand sketch the board swings back into the open space. Next to it is a tall laundry cupboard with a drop-out board. The problem of curtains over swivel-opening windows can be solved by hanging them on a wooden curtain-rod mounted as a swinging bracket on the wall.

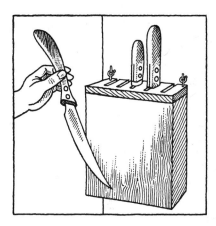

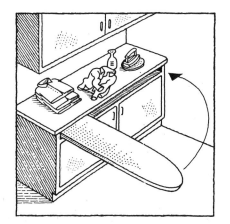

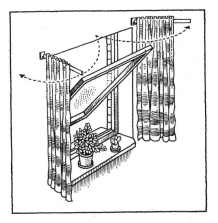

Space for toddlers

Creating space for children in a house or flat which is on the cramped side can be a headache. If each child cannot have a room of its own and there is no space for play in the bedrooms, you may have to give up a corner in the living-room and make it a play area. But this is not essential, for children do not need a great deal of space for play. Maybe all the space you can spare is an area behind the sofa—where there is room for a stool and some cushions, or a little table and chairs. Children are generally crazy about cosy corners or spaces. The playhouse below takes up no more than a square yard (metre) of floor space. The door opening had better be at crawling height for grown-ups.

In a house which is too small, you are particularly aware of the lack of space in cupboards and hallways. The illustrations below and opposite show several solutions to the space problem.

A waist-high cupboard-wall between dining corner and play area provides the children with space for toy storage and mother with a place to put her dishes on the other side. A specially practical point is the transformation of the back of a china cupboard into a blackboard. A folding barrier makes a secure boundary wall.

A simple house of chipboard, assembled on hinges. The house can be held in position with door-hooks, and eyes screwed into the wall. It can be folded away in a small space.

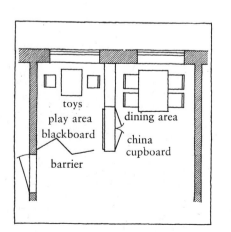

toys
play area
blackboard

dining area

china
cupboard

barrier

A coat-hanger tree from wall to ceiling takes up very little room and offers plenty of storage space. Handy in the hall, but suitable for the nursery as well.

A toy cupboard with a flap for each shelf is easy to keep tidy and seems to hold a lot of things. The hinged flaps have cut-out hand holds.

An old wall cupboard with side hinges can be turned into a handy writing desk. Hang the cupboard sideways on the wall, cut the door away to the desired depth and add chains.

This metal horizontal bar can be removed from the doorway in one movement. It is fitted into two wooden blocks screwed onto the door posts, one with a circular and the other with a U-shaped socket.

Space for the teenager

Only a few teenagers are blessed with a really spacious room. But these sketches show that even a very small room can be made practical and cosy. Incorporating a window into the design of a storage space adds great charm to the finished effect. The window also provides light for the desk area. In the hanging cupboard the space under the clothing is used for small drawers—notice the markers on the drawers. Next to them come the dresses which have to hang full-length.

The right combination of several fresh colours is another important element in creating a room for a teenager.

This cupboard has drawers beneath shelves, affording more space than widely separated shelves would and creating a neater looking cupboard when the door is opened.

A narrow room calls for fixed units. The bed is a simple board with drawers underneath. In the cupboard at the foot of the bed there is space for extra bedding. The holes in the front panel are for ventilation.

A big room divided into two separate compartments—a bookshelf wall and two wardrobe cupboards act as dividers. There are doors on both sides of the cupboard, of which either the left- or the right-hand side can open into the rooms. Cotton-reels are used for doorknobs and pegs.

One and one make two (asleep!)

The bedroom is a chapter in itself. As well as being comfortable and attractive it must above all be practical. Beds which are too low are tiring to make and difficult to clean underneath. Layers of dust can be avoided by using the space under the bed for storage drawers.

A home-made bed-frame of chipboard or blockboard can be folded away in an unused cupboard or niche. The support at the end is hinged to the bed-board. Box beds for two children can be attractively and speciously arranged as shown in the sketch below. This arrangement also gives both children privacy, and they can store some of their possessions in the fixed cupboard between the beds, accessible from both sides. The cupboards above the beds can be fitted with doors hinged at side or with flaps with a piano-lid hinge at the top. The floor of the children's bedroom is left free of furniture and provides ample space for play.

When someone is ill a bed-table can give a lot of pleasure. This one is made of 1 in. (25 mm.) blockboard. The top is 8 in. (20 cm.) longer than the width of the bed, the side panels are 15 in. (40 cm.) higher than the bed. The parts can be glued together, the whole structure painted (white) and wheels attached.

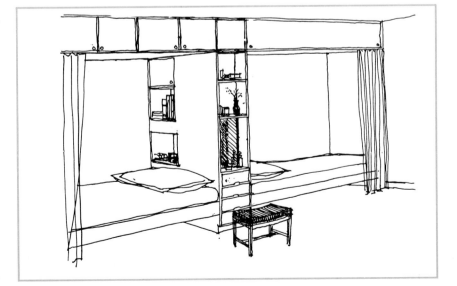

It is important even for a baby to have a place of his own. This is often a problem for young married couples, who may still be living with their parents. Sometimes they haven't even a nook of their own to sleep in, let alone a decent space to put the cot in later on.

If the baby has to sleep in its parents' bedroom, then make a special area for the baby by putting a screen round the cot or cradle, or by hanging a curtain or sunblind from the ceiling. (Remember that paper is apt to be torn by an infant if he can reach it, so beware of thin paper blinds.) Drawstrings to work the curtain or blind should be on a wall near the parental bed, at a safe distance from tiny grabbing hands. Space for changing the baby is sometimes difficult to find. A flap attached to the wall which in its horizontal position drops exactly over the bed solves this problem; but make sure that the child as he grows and is able to stand cannot pull down the flap. Make it safe by fixing two large clips to the wall, into which the flap can be secured, When baby grows up, there may be some brothers and sisters. Anyone living in a small house or flat will have to put several children in one room. This can cause space problems, which can usually be solved with imagination and thought.

A screen designed for a cot is framed with wooden bars. The panels of the screen can be made from material stretched between the wooden frame, or coloured cardboard, or raffia, or wooden slats framed on all sides.

Bunks beds are an ideal way of saving space, and they can be built and arranged in different ways so that the least possible space is wasted.
If you choose one or more fold-away beds, remember that they combine best with fixed furniture. Avoid spending every evening pushing chairs and tables out of the way after playtime. A flap-table is handy as a desk in the bedroom. A lift-up seat—perhaps with a storage bin underneath—is a convenient chair. Clothes usually dropped on chairs and the floor seem less messy if they hang on hooks and hangers attached to the wall. For discarded socks and underclothes, make flowered cotton bags, which can also hang on the wall.

Good ventilation is important in a room where several children are sleeping. A small skylight does not usually supply enough ventilation especially as it must sometimes be shut because of strong winds. A window or wall ventilator or an extra air grid in the outside wall provides a good and draught-proof solution.

This small bedroom for parents and baby has been very sensibly arranged. The baby's bed can also be a playpen, and the space next to it can be used as a working surface. Storage space is available in the deep clothes cupboard to the right and underneath baby's worktop-playpen-bed.

Three stacked beds in the space of two. The third bed—pushed between the other two—can be pulled out as far as necessary at night. It is set on castors for this purpose.

Three small bunks in a narrow room— arranged so that each child still has enough air over its head. The beds are bolted to the wall and screwed to the centre post, which has stilt treads for climbing.

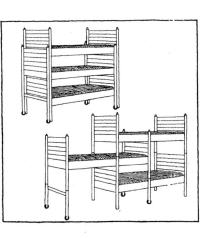

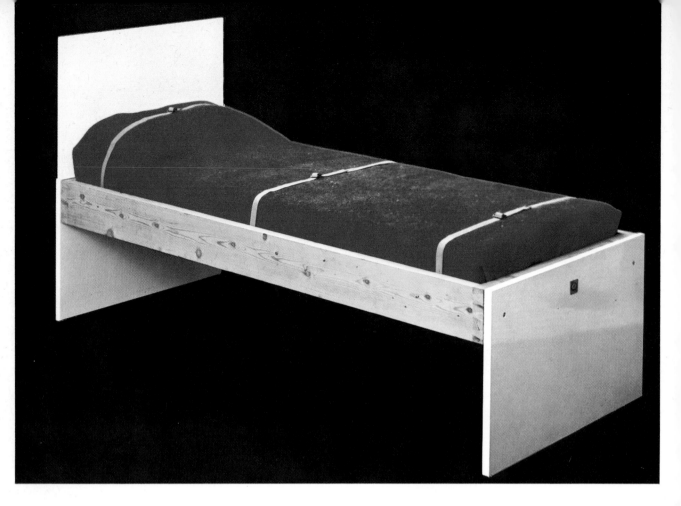

Dreaming over a playground

This bed-frame swivels between two fixed end-boards (1) so that the underside of the bed can be used as a play surface during the day. Be sure to have the bed in a fixed position for the necessary stability, and screw wall-board (j) to the wall. Then screw one of the bed-ends (c) onto the wall-board, leaving some of the wall-board to project a little above the bed-end in order to give support to the head-board. Above this section screw wall-board (m), supported on wall-board (n), which is also fixed to the wall. The oblique edges ensure a good lock. In the centre of both ends of the bed-frame drill a $\frac{3}{8}$ in. (10 mm.) hole for a bolt. Do the same—measure the exact position carefully—in the bed-ends. Then fix a square metal plate between the bed-end and the frame-end—exactly over the drilled holes—and insert another plate inside the frame-end. Slide bolt through wooden pieces and into lock and locknut. Diagram 3 shows how the straps should be inserted behind the aluminium strip.

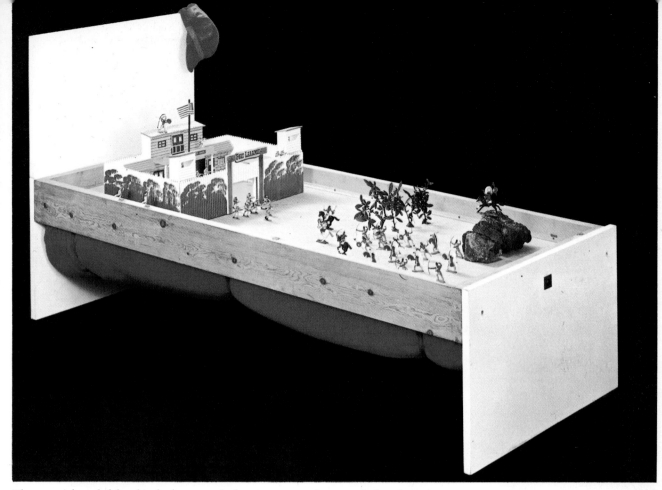

The material needed for this dual-purpose bed are:

   a 2 planed deal planks for the long sides of the bed-frame (76 × 6 × 1½ in.) (195 × 15 × 4 cm.)

   b the same for the short sides (32 × 6 × 1½ in.) (81 × 15 × 4 cm.)

c and k 3 pieces of blockboard (⅞ in.) (22 mm.) for bed-ends, and head-board (32 × 20 in.) (81 × 51 cm.)

   d 4 square metal plates 1½ × 1½ in. (4 × 4 cm.) with a ⅜ in. (10 mm.) hole in the middle, and 2 bolts (⅜ in., 3 in. long) (10 mm., 8 cm. long) with nut and locknut, for the revolving mechanism

   e 3 lengths of webbing 1 in. (3 cm.) wide with buckles, to hold the bedding and mattress in place

   f 2 aluminium angle strips (66 × ¾ × ¾ in.) (168 × 1.5 × 1.5 cm) with flat-headed screws 1 in. (2 cm.) long to hold mattress and webbing (see fig. 3)

   g ½ in. (10 mm.) blockboard or plywood to fit into bed-frame

   h 4 dowels ½ in. (10 mm.) in diameter and 4 in. (10 cm.) long, with nylon thread and eye screws for the bed-frame

j,m,n, 3 deal wall planks (20 × 3 × 1in .) (51 × 7 × 2.5 cm), two of them with bevelled edges, to attach to the wall and bed-ends

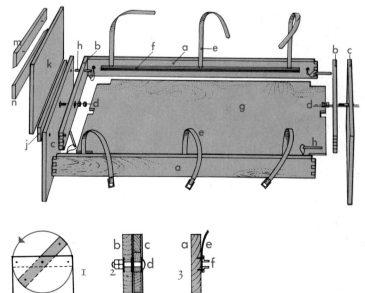

A bunk, a wall and a roll of wallpaper

The subjects of 'sleep' and 'play' have a good many more ideas to offer than have yet been considered, so here are two more pages with various suggestions.

What boy would not dream about a bed like this one, set high in a wall niche like a ship's berth? The wall bars combine two functions, those of ladder and amusing play apparatus.

If brother and sister have to share a room there are problems—but not if you use a high bunk to create a partition which divides the room in two.

Bunks are the order of the day. Little 'top-sleepers' need a strong high barrier to keep them from falling out of bed. To make it easier to climb in and out of bed, the barrier should be a flap on piano hinges with bolts to hold it up in position during the night.

In small houses improvisation is needed when the time comes for friends to spend the night. In the sketch opposite a two-bunk sleeping area is made by fixing a 50 in. (130 cm.) width of blockboard above the lower bunk. The blockboard should fold in half on piano hinges, so that it can also serve as a shelf for storing toys.

Play

The outside of a cupboard door can be painted with blackboard paint for a small child. When the child outgrows blackboard drawing, the door can quite simply be painted over with ordinary paint.

A roll of paper is ideal for children who want to live creatively. First

fix a piece of board to the wall, and onto this attach a rod to hold the roll of paper. To hold the paper in place and tear it off at the bottom, attach two long metal strips to the board.

A good enclosed tray on four legs can be made of left-over rods of wood. To avoid splinters planing, sand-papering and painting are desirable. Then even city children may get a chance to play with sand on the balcony or in their own rooms.

Rockabye baby

A view from above shows that the pram body fits quite loosely in its container.

Why should a cot always have legs, or wheels, or a canopy? It could be something completely different, as you can see from the illustrations here. This cheerful and useful cradle is made of heavy canvas and is designed as a container for a pram top or carry-cot. The measurements given here provide ample space for a pram top measuring 32 × 15 in. (83 × 39 cm.). The round poles (1 in., 22 mm., in diameter) measure 37 in. (95 cm.) for the sides and 20 in. (51 cm.) across each end. They should be rounded off at the ends and a quarter of the thickness cut away 1 in. (2.5 cm.) from the end, so that the poles fit securely against each other. Holes must be drilled through the poles, so that they can be held together with ring bolts.

For good suspension, it is advisable to attach the hanging ropes to a crossbar ½ in. (10 mm.) in diameter (*see* drawing below). This bar also allows a net to be hung over the cradle as protection against insects and falling leaves.

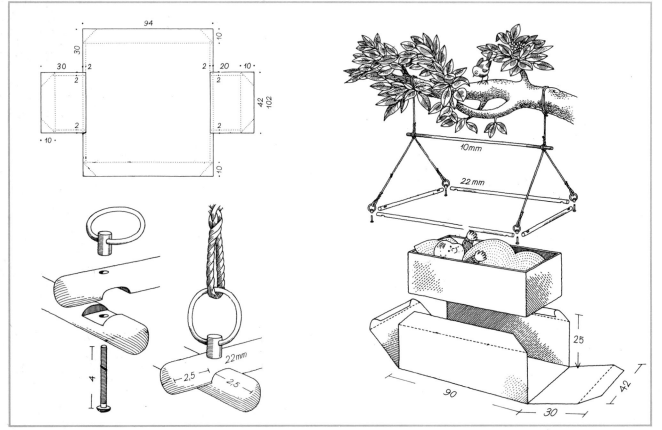

A yellow cradle like this looks especially nice when hanging in a garden. Striped canvas also gives a colourful effect. Baby is safer in a hanging cradle than when the detachable pram top is supported on a couple of chairs or a table. The hanging cradle is airier than a pram.

A little place in the country

If your outdoor home life is limited to a balcony it is important to use the very small space as efficiently as possible. A balcony on the sunny side of a building calls for an awning. A projecting balcony catches a lot of wind, especially on the higher floors of a tower block, and we show you how to make a storm-proof awning (*see* instructions in caption below).

You can furnish a balcony with fixed or folding benches, and you could use the balcony rail to attach a table-flap. A miniature garden with toy houses and/or a small fountain add decoration and provide amusement for the children.

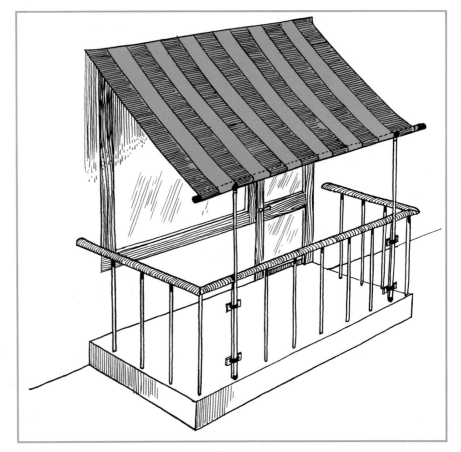

Attach two broomsticks to the balcony rails with clamps, and protect the ends of the stick with plastic caps. Make two 'button-holes' in the awning canvas where the pole and supporting broomsticks meet. Pull a piece of wire through the holes and twist round awning pole and broomstick.

64

A table-flap can be made in various ways
—for instance, attach a slatted frame to
two metal hooks which fit over the
balcony railing (*see* sketch). If you are
using left-over slats for the flap, make
sure that the upper surfaces are smooth.
A glass of lemonade or a cup of milk
upsets so easily. You may prefer to buy
a slatted frame and the brackets in a
hardware or garden shop. Some brackets
hook over the railing and can be attached
to the vertical posts with screws. These
brackets have two fold-away metal
supports, and the table-top rests on
these. Remember that non-weatherproof
tables and chairs must be protected
against bad weather or taken indoors
when it rains. Tables made of plastic-
coated chipboard (on both surfaces)
usually do well outdoors, as long as the
strip along the edges is carefully treated
with waterproof adhesive.
In the drawing to the right we have
sketched the design for a table which
can rest on its side on the balcony rail,
held in place by ropes and hooks. Of

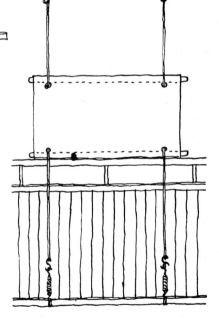

course the materials used have to be
thoroughly wind and weather proof.
The table-top is supported on its long
sides by two bars. One of these rests on
the balcony rail and faces outside when
the table-top is on its side. In the upper
support bar (*see* sketch) we have drilled
two holes 2–4 in. (5–10 cm.) from the
ends. When the table-top is to be let
down and used, two steel bars are inserted into these holes and become table
legs, if necessary to be linked together
for greater stability.

Nature indoors and out

Gardening as a hobby should not degenerate into hard labour. So why not leave the days of impeccable lawns and tidy flowerbeds behind and organize the garden for the modern man? A number of interesting details like stones and pieces of wood should be included in today's garden to help create a balanced design and leave space for adults and children to play.

In most gardens the accent is on the greenery and the flowers. But an area of hard 'floor' should be part of the garden as a place for sitting and playing, walking or riding bicycles on. This floor should add interest, and can be made from a variety of stones or tiles which are now available. As well as natural stone, such as sandstone and flagstones, there are concrete and hard-burnt bricks and tiles. Be careful about soft tiles and bricks, for they are liable to crack in frost, or they may grow moss, with all the obvious consequences. All types of stone and brick offer their own advantages for laying out artistic patterns or simply for accentuating the natural beauty of the stones and their irregularities. Not for the patio, but for the drive or parking area there are also various kinds of grits and gravels; but these materials have to be renewed about every four years.

Here are eleven designs for laying out a 'garden floor' made of hard-burnt building bricks. In the first six variations the broad side of the brick is uppermost and in the next five the narrow edge. The second method calls for twice as many bricks as the first.

Cobble-stones can be used as a floor covering in the garden. 'Genuine' ones are rather pricey; but there are simulated cobble-stones made of concrete. If you happen to know of a cobble-stone street which is to be torn up, try to buy up the stones. Besides being less expensive, they will have been rubbed smooth by use.

Hexagonal tiles for a path or the patio. Here grass has been left in the gaps; on the terrace you could grow flowers in the gaps.

A sound tile floor is laid like this: grub up the earth to a depth of 4–6 in. (10–15 cm.) plus the thickness of the tiles. Spread a layer of gravel 4 in. (10 cm.) deep, covered by a 2 in. (5 cm.) layer of loam sand. Roll or stamp down the layers and level off the surface with a plank. Stretch strings across the area to be covered to mark the height of the tiles themselves. Lay the tiles one by one, hammer them home with a wooden mallet and check with a spirit level to see that they are even. Tiles can be joined simply by using jointing pins which are made to measure and are placed between the tiles to ensure they are lying correctly. After laying, brush grouting into the joints.

68

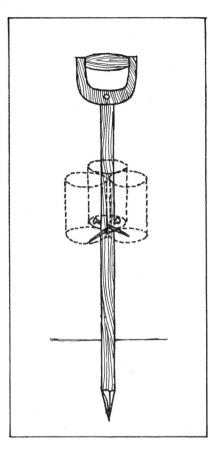

Stick this handy garden gadget into the ground beside you and everything is to hand, leaving hands free. The tins rest on two long nails hammered cross-wise through the handle and are held together with a piece of strong tape.

The useful tool becomes a handsome present if you paint the tins and put some flowers in them.

Try to emphasize the natural characteristics of sandstone. The shape and colour of every piece should be an integral part of the over-all design. Laying out a large area requires patience.

Ideas for an entrance

In the front garden, even an unenthusiastic gardener can express his individuality. The three front gardens to the right show how this can be done. The areas are exactly the same size, they lie side-by-side on the same road and belong to the same sort of house, but there all resemblance ends. More about these three front gardens and the six gardens below, on page 72.

This front garden is still very new. In time the ground-cover plants will form a more intimate unity with the ornamental stones.

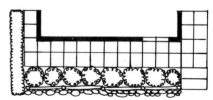

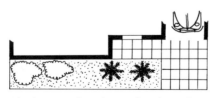

A friendly sort of garden with about 1,000 flowers behind a fence of pine trunks.

The front garden of a modern bungalow, straightforward, well thought-out and planned to look cool.

A wealth of flowers, a rustic fence, the cosiness which suits a farm.

The well-clipped privet hedge round this paved front garden gives the occupants privacy without depriving the rooms of light.

A fairly open garden, affording residents and passers-by a view of flowering plants and roses against the green of berberis.

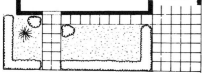

Cheap and simple to maintain was the idea behind the design of this front garden.

Two plant troughs give character to this entrance.

Small tiles, small-leaved bushes, small grass plots—you can fit a whole lot in that way.

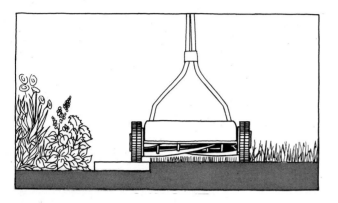

Grass which grows where it shouldn't is prevented from spreading into flower beds by a tile edging. This also makes it a little easier to keep the grass edges straight with the mower.

An empty tin is useful when you are planting bulbs in turf. Press the tin into the grass, open end downwards, and bore a neat hole. Pop the bulb in and cover it up again with earth.

A more detailed description follows of the front gardens on the previous pages. They are described in the following order: first the three front gardens in the top row, from left to right; then the six in the bottom row, also from left to right.
A glance at the illustrations of the top three shows you that there can be quite a difference between front gardens with the same dimensions. In the first garden, red and green berberis and between the stones 'cushion-forming' plants, which together make up a mosaic. In the second garden the privet hedge creates an intimate atmosphere inside, which is missing from a more open front garden. The flowering plant box under the window supplies some colour. In the third garden, Japanese cherry, red and yellow roses with blue lavender. An evergreen berberis adds some colour in the winter.
Bottom Row: the first front garden blends with the rural surroundings in which the house stands— plenty of flowers and a pine fence (with the bark still on it), with wind- and water-proofed posts.

Next to it a very cool garden. A double course of flagstones forms the one barrier between grass and pavement. Birches and ordinary Christmas trees in the garden. One disadvantage here is the easy access for litter and dogs. The garden around a rustic farm (your country cottage?) can be free and easy. A mass of flowers is important: bulbs, asters, jasmine, clematis, climbing roses. All this calls for a hedge or, as here, a secure fence. Next to it, a lawn, surrounded by dwarf pines and yellow potentilla, which grows in any type of soil and flowers in both sun and shade from May to October. In the next garden a healthy balance has been struck between plants and stones. Cobbles on the ground, and in the strongly-built plant troughs, weigelia and dogwood. In the last front garden the driveway is at a higher level than the tiled path to the front door. The shallow steps connecting the different levels give the garden a playful character, emphasized by *Lonicera nitida*, a delicate-leaved bush, which has to be pruned in spring because the tips of the branches freeze in winter.

A vertical garden

The hardy annuals, with their wealth of blooms which crowd the established plants in a flower border, are best suited to this flower stand or 'stacked border'. It can divide up or enclose the terrace, or it can be placed where one can see it from indoors as well. The stacked border is not difficult to make. Two sheets of waterproof plywood form the sections, as shown in the diagram on the left. The stand is 48 in. (122 cm.) high, the troughs 6 in. (15 cm.) deep, with a distance of 8 in. (20 cm.) between them. After sawing the pieces of plywood, begin to nail the various sections together. Mark on both sides where the shelves should be: then attach them, starting with the bottom shelf, $\frac{3}{4}$ in. (2 cm.) clear of the ground. The upper ones follow. Use $1\frac{1}{2}$ – 2 in. (40 – 50 mm.) galvanized nails. Finally, paint the stand with a wood preservative. Overleaf is a stacked border in all its glory.

Sawing plan for the stacked border, which is self-explanatory. Use one sheet of $\frac{1}{2}$ in, (16 mm.) plywood measuring 48 × 100 in. (122 × 254 cm.) and one of 26 × 48 in. (65 × 122 cm.).

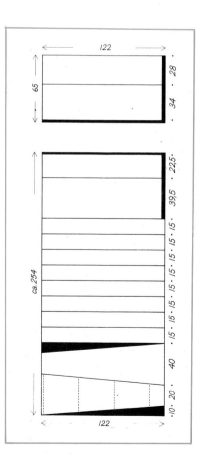

73

Playing with flowers

A 'stacked border', filled here with pansies, fuchsias, dwarf french marigolds, petunias and mesembryanthemum is handy for the gardener who is past the age of easy stooping. He can tend these plants while standing upright.

Who can resist a field of summer flowers, asking to be picked, begging to be enjoyed? Wreath-weaving, for instance, is a flower game which we recall, but how did it actually go, that ingenious weaving? There are four photographs on page 76 to remind you. If instead you want to leave the flowers undisturbed in the meadows, you can grow 'everlasting' flowers in your own garden to pick and make into wreaths and bouquets for the winter. There is a rich selection of flowers for this purpose, described on page 77.

Picked in the summer, kept for the winter, wreaths made from dried 'everlasting' flowers.

(1) The left hand holds, the right hand ties. The long stem of the first flower acts as a guide in the weaving. The photographs show how the stem of the second flower is curled round the guide stem, pulled to the front of the flower-head and laid parallel to the first stem. (2) The third flower is woven round two stems, the fourth round three stems, etc. Stems which have

already had several others woven round them can be clipped off as required. (3) The wreath is closed by weaving the stems of the last two flowers back through the beginning of the circle, (4) and drawing the last flowers gently towards the first. You can also weave with several flowers at a time, making a thicker wreath.

Picking flowers for the winter

The summer gives us an abundance of flowers, many of which can be dried for winter bouquets to remind us of summer even on the dreariest days of January and February when the price of cut flowers in the florist shops is at its highest. Why not spend the last few days of high summer in the garden and the fresh air, looking for suitable flowers for drying? If your children want to go 'harvesting' as well, explain to them about roots and point out that picking flowers will soon be a thing of the past if the underground part of the plant is picked as well. Your own garden could supply a harvest of dried flowers—globe thistle and cow parsnip *(Heracleum spondylium)*, achilleas and common catmint, astilbes and the various ornamental grasses can all be included in the dried-flower bouquet. And of course the ever popular annual immortelles must not be forgotten. It is very easy to grow them. Perhaps you could reserve a special place in the garden for these flowers for the winter—at the back, for instance, so that you don't denude the garden when you pick them. Mixed immortelle seed can be bought in small packets with instructions for use.

Flat-dwellers can also pick flowers for the winter. A stroll in the country can provide a variety of 'everlasting flowers'—bullrushes, reeds, elegant grasses and ferns. Distinctive twigs and striking pods can also be included in the dried bouquet. Very attractive, and well worth drying are the pods of columbine and larkspur, peony and poppy and the familiar honesty.

Picking and Drying

If you have honesty in the garden, the seed pods should be picked early when they first appear about July. Generally, flowers you want to dry are best picked in full bloom. Unopened buds have a tendency to droop during the drying and make a cheerless impression in the winter bouquet. Immortelles (Helichrysum) or everlasting, are ready to be picked the moment their yellow hearts are about to open. This is the flower's signal that the seed is about to form and it should not be allowed to go any further, because once this happens, the flower becomes less durable. Branches with ornamental pods must also be picked before the seeds have fully ripened, otherwise there will be little left on bough or stalk by the time they are dried. Twigs and flowers can be dried either singly or in big bunches. The most beautiful results are achieved in a dry, warm, dark cupboard where there is good air

circulation. Tie flowers up in small bunches and leave them hanging upside-down. Some twigs, however, will be better if they are left to stand in a vase, so that the stems do not become too stiff and brittle. This applies to the umbelliferous plants such as cow parsnip and parsley. With astilbes and catmint the leaves should also be removed before drying, because they are not attractive when preserved. Ferns with their large, flat leaves are particularly suited to being pressed, even though they are difficult to handle when dried. Pick ferns in September, just before they turn yellow, and dry them individually between layers of absorbent paper (blotting or newspaper) placed under a heavy weight, like a pile of books. Leave the ferns undisturbed for about four weeks, when they are ready to take their place in the winter bouquet. Dry the immortelles in bunches upside-down, after removing all the leaves. Pick ornamental grasses while they are still slightly green, and dry them standing in vases so that they do not lose their natural graceful shape. The big reeds and rushes picked on a walk along the river are especially decorative, but are a nuisance unless they have been properly prepared beforehand. Spray these twigs and seeds with hair lacquer which 'preserves' them and keeps everything in place.

The winter bouquet can be quite simply dried by standing the flowers—astilbes, ornamental grasses and cow parsnip, for instance—immediately after picking, in a vase filled with clay or sand. The result is a bouquet which is striking for its natural charm.

A miniature 'bottled' garden

In dry, centrally heated rooms, it is sometimes difficult to keep house plants healthy during the winter. Why not try putting a plant in a bottle? Start with a small plant and a bit of patience. With a narrow-necked bottle, the planting process is as follows: on the bottom of the bottle spread one layer of gravel or sand mixed with fine peat or potter's clay, making sure that these materials are bone-dry so that they don't stick to the sides of the bottle. The next step is to take two bamboo planting sticks and put your small plant on the stick with the split end. Carefully guide the plant or cutting to the bottom of the bottle, where you have meanwhile dug a small hole with the other stick. Set the cutting down and press the earth in well round the roots. After planting give the plant a little water.

Even though bottle gardens are becoming increasingly popular, there is still a place for cut flowers in most homes. Here are five devices for holding your flower arrangements upright and in position.
1. A frame made of two layers of chicken wire, secured to the sides of the vase by three wire hooks 1½ in. (4 cm.) apart.
2. A wedge of Oasis fits perfectly. Stiff stalks are pushed through it and remain neatly in place. 3. A really natural solution. Take a sturdy twig which you can find lying about in a garden or woods and fix it firmly in a glass or vase. 4. and 5. To avoid the problem of heavy flower arrangements toppling over, put pretty marbles or coloured stones on the bottom of the vase and move the centre of gravity to this base. Stiff stalks or twigs can be stuck between the marbles or pebbles.

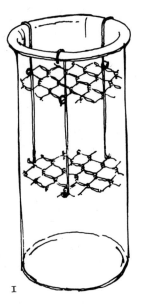

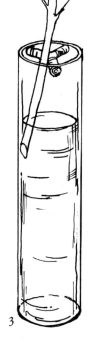

1   2   3   4   5

The success of a pretty
bottlegarden lies in the fact
that the perfect climate can
be created inside the bottle
for a 'warm-blooded'
plant: in the wine carboy,
a maranta (prayer plant);
in the twin brandy glasses
a violet; and genuinely
'bottled', a fern (Pteris
cretica).

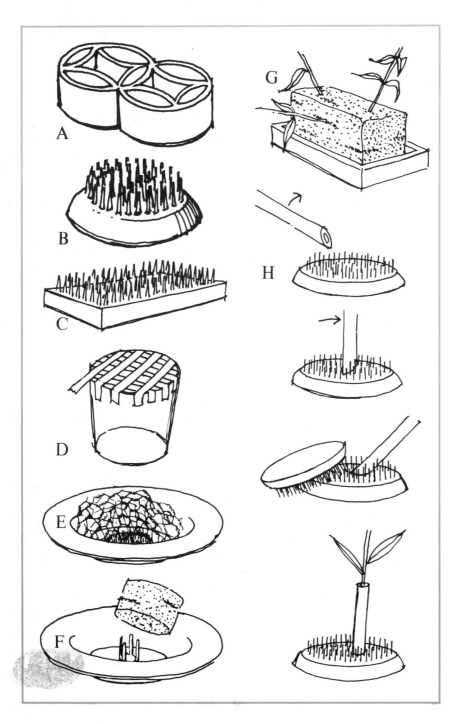

Bases of flower arranging

Flowers set in low bowls or shallow troughs can be very unusual and pleasing, whether they are arranged in round bunches or more sparsely like a Japanese flower arrangement. There are a number of types of holders known as frogs. Sketch A shows a design for very thick stalks. The pin-head frogs (B, C, H) will certainly be familiar to you. They are available in all sizes, round, oblong, square, with thin or thick, long or short spikes. But if you are unable to find a really thin one for fragile flower stems, you can improvise by taking a thick, hollow stalk into which you can slip a thinner one (H). Then wedge the whole thing firmly between the spikes of a pin-head frog. You can make a holder yourself from fine mesh chicken wire (E) which you mould into a hemisphere and bind together with wire. For extra stability place a flat stone inside the chicken wire and place the side of the holder with the stone in it on the bottom of the bowl or press it firmly into plastic clay. A chicken-wire holder can also stand on a pin-head frog. A short tumbler (D) can be transformed into a flower container by 'weaving' sticky tape over the top. A disadvantage of this method is that the sticky tape comes off as soon as it gets wet. Don't forget round and square sections of Oasis for flower arranging, and the special Oasis holders.

Almost any bottle can be used as a mini-garden. Old-fashioned sweet bottles and chemists' bottles are particularly suitable. The best indoor plants to grow in bottles are *Sansevieria*, *Dracaena*, *Maranta*, friesia, *Peperomia*, *Pilea*, *Tolmiea* (Pickaback), and of course the ferns. It is best to move the plants to the bottle when they are still in the tender seedling stage. You could also experiment by planting a miniature woodland in a bottle—some moss, a little fern, and wild grasses. Then add an acorn or beechnut —they really do germinate.

Until the plants in a bottle garden grow too tall, you can keep a cork in the top of the bottle. Remove the cork to give the plants an airing, but make sure that the earth in the bottle is always slightly damp. Evaporation keeps the humidity in the bottle at the right level for the plants. A constant mist in the bottle is a danger signal, for it means there is too much humidity and the plants run the risk of rotting.

83

Watch them grow

When a pip comes to life in a pot of earth and a plant begins to grow, a child can become involved in the 'miracle of nature' right in his own room. Peas and beans, for instance, develop while you watch. Put them in lukewarm water so they can 'pump' themselves full; and in a few days roots and leaves will already be growing. Later on the plants can be moved to the garden or the windowbox. Sweet corn lends itself to the same sort of experiment, but is easily outpaced by mustard and cress, which can be sown on damp blotting paper, and left for about three days in a darkish, damp, warm place. When the seeds have germinated you can bring the plant back to the light of day. Oats, birdseed and grass can also be sown in little dishes. Radishes, all sorts of colza and marigolds should be left in darkness for three days after sowing, then returned to the light quickly before they wilt. The pips of dates, oranges, lemons and grapefruit will often sprout in a pot of damp

An ordinary onion, given the same treatment as its chic relation the hyacinth, develops in an amazingly short time into a big green plant. Fill a hyacinth pot or an ordinary glass jar with water and put the onion on top, making sure that the flat underside of the onion touches the water. In a few days roots will appear, and after a week green leaves will begin to grow.

Slice off the tops of carrots and beets, place in a dish of water; and they will form leaves and flowers.

Oats in a bowl.

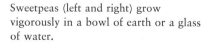

Sweetpeas (left and right) grow vigorously in a bowl of earth or a glass of water.

earth on the window-sill. But you must wait three weeks before you begin to see a green plant. Nuts will do the same thing. It is just as easy as it looks here. Let your children make the discovery for themselves, let them do the planting and watch their plants growing.

Know your house plants

Although by nature they are used to something quite different, a reasonable number of plants—mostly of tropical origin—will adapt very well to the west European sitting room. Nevertheless, you will have to go half-way to meet some rather individual 'nursing requirements', and unfortunately, there are no universal rules for the cultivation of house plants. You know yourself from experience that what is good for one plant does another no good at all. The origin of a plant plays an important role in its care, so if you know where it originally came from, you should have greater success in caring for each plant in your home. Knowing how plants grow and flower in their natural surroundings will help you to arrange things to suit them indoors. Some house plants betray at a glance the surroundings which appeal to them most. The cacti, with their built-in reservoirs of water, are typical desert plants, and the leathery, heat-resistant leaves of the *Sansevieria* point to a life in the sun. It is not so easy to tell from looking at a *Begonia* that it was originally cultivated in the subtropics. The lack of humidity—especially in centrally-heated flats and houses—is a problem for most plants. Unless you are growing cacti or foliage plants which can withstand dry air, you must take steps to increase the humidity around the plants. Although it is sometimes recommended to place a saucer of water in front of a radiator, this does very little to increase the general moisture level in the atmosphere. To increase the humidity around the plant, stand it on an upturned saucer in a basin of water. As the water evaporates it transmits moisture to the air immediately round the plant.

Cacti and succulents grow well in a light east or west window. Warmth and light suit them in summer, but in winter they should be kept in light but cool conditions (40°F) (6°C). Cacti which spend the winter in a heated room get out of step and forget to flower at all. Cool becomes too cool if they are left in an unheated room at night between the glass and the tightly drawn curtains. This also applies generally to house plants. The risk of freezing on a window-sill is considerable and house plants do not easily survive a temperature below freezing.

A home playground

The nicest sandpit for a child is a great heap of loose sand somewhere in the corner of the garden, where he can play to his heart's content. But most gardens are not big enough to accomodate a sand heap of this type, and many gardeners would cast anxious glances at all the sand drifts which would inevitably spill over onto their lawns. A sandpit which knows its own limitations can be made like this. The simplest way is to drive posts about 2 ft. (60 cm.) long into the ground for the four corners. To these you attach four planks for the sides (with countersunk nails). The planks should be treated beforehand with wood preservative. Inside this square frame dig out a layer of earth and spread a 4 in. (10 cm.) drainage layer of gravel. If the sandpit is meant for vigorous diggers, it is advisable to sink the side walls into the ground and also to lay a fixed floor of tiles or planks (which again are treated with wood preservative). To keep the sandpit from becoming water-logged, you must also provide a drainage hole. The sketches on these two pages show a de-luxe model sandpit. Two of the sides have seats which serve as covers for storage places for toys, pails, spades, etc. A sandpit like this one, with a fixed floor and a drain could also be used

A sandpit does not have to be dug in; it can also be a big wooden box, which can be moved about and even brought inside (in the latter situation remember to put a tarpaulin on the floor to trap the sand which trickles through). There are no particular limitations on the size of a sandpit as long as a child and his friend can play in it without getting in each other's way.

on a balcony. In the garden it is best to have a sandpit in a place where the children can be seen from the house. It should, if possible, be in a sunny, sheltered spot where a shade from the sun could also be rigged. Small children get sunstroke much more easily than we realise. The best sand to use is beach sand. Unlike sharp sand, this is not sticky and will not cling to the children's clothes when it becomes damp, or blow about when it dries. Don't worry about providing completely dry sand; in a slightly damp condition it is great fun to play with. A covering for the sandpit can be very useful to shelter it from showers and falling leaves and to protect against 'beasties' and roving cats which regard the sand as a highly desirable lavatory.

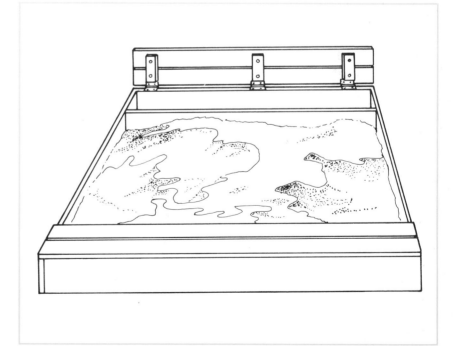

Playing about with water is perhaps even more fun for a child than playing with sand. The sketch shows how to build a knock-down paddling pool. Any father with a carpenter's eye will be able to build this. The frame is constructed of tongue-and-groove deal planks ($\frac{1}{2}$ × 5 in.) (3 × 12.5 cm.): four 8 ft. (244 cm.) lengths for the long sides and four 5 ft. 6 in. (167 cm.) lengths for the short sides.

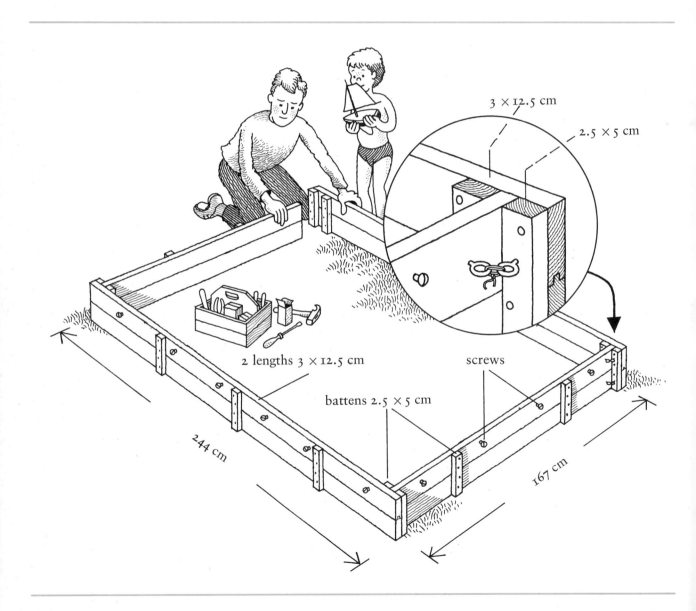

3 × 12.5 cm

2.5 × 5 cm

2 lengths 3 × 12.5 cm

screws

battens 2.5 × 5 cm

244 cm

167 cm

Eighteen 1 × 2 in. (2.5 × 5 cm.) battens hold the frame together, as the sketch shows. These are held together by 1½ in. (3.5 cm.) galvanized nails. Eyelet screws and strong rope—see a close-up of the construction in the circular diagram— hold the corners together. The sketch also shows round-headed screws projecting from the outside of the planks. These are used to hold a plastic-canvas lining in place. 'Coated' canvas can be stuck together with a contact adhesive into a sheet measuring 10 ft 10 in. × 8 ft. 6 in. (3.30 × 2.60 m.). Into the doubled edges of the sheet you can put canvas eyelets. Then just add water and let the children splash.

An ingenious idea, shown above, enables two children of unequal weight to see-saw together in balance. The fulcrum of the see-saw can be moved to alter the lever action of the apparatus according to the weight of the children. You can see this in the photo (right). Neither has the advantage in weight, which prevents accidental bumps and falls. This should help to save a good many teeth and noses.

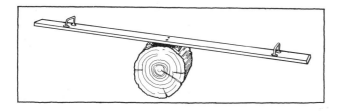

A plank with two handrails, nailed to a solid piece of tree-trunk, makes a splendid see-saw.

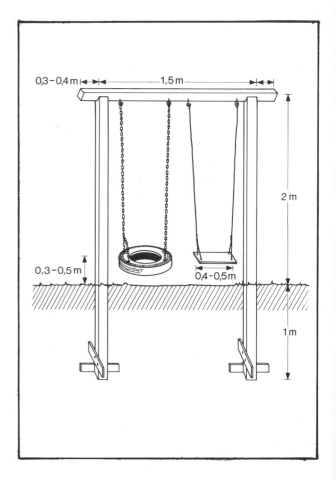

The swing shown in the drawing and photo on the left is supported by 4 × 4 in. (10 × 10 cm.) beams. The uprights are 10 ft. (3 m.) in length, the cross-beam 5 ft. (1.50 m.). The uprights are dug in to a depth of 3 ft. (1 m.) and stabilized at the bottom with cross supports 2 × 4 in. (5 × 10 cm.), length about 2 ft. (60 cm.). The cross supports are attached with 5 in. (12 cm.) galvanized nails. As shown in the sketch, the cross-beam at the top is laid in a fork cut in the uprights and anchored by 3 in. (7.5 cm.) galvanized nails. Be sure to treat the timber used with a wood preservative; and use genuine swing hooks to hang the equipment, otherwise the children will swing themselves off the stand. On a swing hanging from chains, slip a length of garden hose over the chain at hand height for a better grip. If you are using rope, splice the top round a steel thimble (obtainable from a ship-chandler).

A swing usually hangs from a tall stand; but it could also hang from the strongest branch of big tree.

Make a deck-chair seat removable (and washable) by pushing rods through the upper and lower seams to keep the cover in place, as the sketch shows.

Puppets, drums and dressing-up

Want to make yourself a Punch and Judy show? Or a crazy wig? Or a set of musical instruments?

You can, with a little help from
Mum and Dad, which they'll be
only too glad to give.

How to make puppets

Take an empty beer bottle (you are going to make the puppet's head on this). Mix up plenty of wallpaper paste. Fit an empty toilet-paper roll, covered with paste, over the neck of the bottle. Shred old newspapers into strips and have scissors and paintbrush ready.

Crumple some newspaper strips into a ball—that's for the puppet's head—and put the ball on top of the roll. Brush some paste on one of the strips of newspaper.

Now you have to fix the head on the roll. Don't use gummed paper because it's not waterproof. Use a strip of newspaper, binding it with paste once or twice over the head and the roll.

Fix the head on even more firmly by sticking some more pasted strips of paper over it and then a few more, crosswise, until it is really sitting firmly.

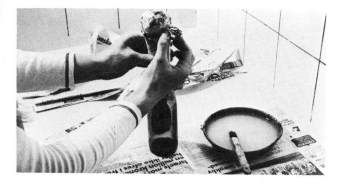

Now it's time for the nose. Make it from a small ball of newspaper. Put some paste on it and press against the head. Oh, you may get a bit of paste on your clothes, but don't worry, a little water will remove it.

To make the nose a little stronger, cut some narrower strips of newspaper, brush them with paste, stick them over the nose and the head. Make the ears in the same way as the nose and fix them on in the same way, too.

Now add a few more criss-cross pasted strips over the head to thicken it a little, and thoroughly daub it all with paste again. Now mould the head into shape a little.

Take a good look at this photograph. Cut out a piece of paper and paste it over the head, leaving holes for the puppet's nose, neck and ears, When the head is completely dry you can paint and varnish it: the examples on the earlier pages will give you some ideas.

Which came first (the owl or the eggbox)?

Collect some of the things which are probably thrown away at home: plastic bowls that once held margarine, boxes and bottles of all shapes and sizes, kitchen rolls, used wrapping paper and those handy egg boxes. And make sure you have lots of paint in every possible colour. Do you like the owl best? Take two egg boxes: one for six eggs and one for a dozen. Now take some sheets of drawing paper, paste, poster-paint and strong scissors or a knife. You make the owl's head by sticking the top and bottom of the six-egg box together. Make the owl's body in the same way, but first cut off the last two projections ('egg-cups') of the box, as these will be used to make the owl's feet. Now the owl's wings: paint some drawing paper and cut out the wings and give them a 'toothed' edge as in the photograph. Now paint the owl in the colours you yourself like best, and when all the paint is dry stick your owl together.

Next you have to perch the owl on the tree. For the tree you need one long tube (the kind used to hold a rolled-up poster or calendar) and some kitchen or toilet-paper rolls. With a knife or scissors make some horizontal cuts in the big tube and fit the other rolls into them. Paint the trunk and branches. Now paint a sheet of paper green and cut out the leaves for the tree.

For the racing car with drivers you will need a six-egg box and the centre of a kitchen roll (or two toilet-paper rolls), scissors, paste, paint and varnish. Use the top of the egg box for the body of each car. For the front take two of the projections from the underside of the box, and leave them joined together. Two more 'egg-cups' become the heads of the racing drivers. Cut them out and stick them together. You can use more egg-cups for the headlamps; and you can make wheels from slices of the kitchen or toilet-paper rolls with wrappingpaper stuck over the ends. Paint all the 'spare parts' before you stick them on the car. Give the car a coat of varnish when everything is dry and set firmly.

To make the pretty dolls-in-a-box you will need two six-egg boxes, paste, paint and varnish. If you take a good look at the photograph at the bottom right of this page, you will see just how to stick the boxes together: you can puzzle it out. Once you've got it all right, paint in the dolls' faces, arms and so forth. And again, varnish when dry.

Your private band

If you enjoy making a loud noise—and your parents can bear it!—you will find everything to your liking on the next four pages. All you need is some old junk to make your own 'musical instruments'. Your next birthday party will be a roaring success with your own band!

Take an old comb, for instance. You can make an impressive sort of humming noise with that. This is what you do: fold a piece of greaseproof paper—or strong tissue paper—over the comb. And then just hum with the comb against your mouth.

Two saucepan lids—preferably not mother's newest—banged together produce a cymbal-like sound.

Perhaps mother has one of those old washboards tucked away in some cupboard, otherwise you can always try granny, or an old aunt or neighbour. Then you must get hold of 5 thimbles, one for each finger. Run them over the washboard and the most wonderful sound emerges.

For this instrument you need a good matchbox and some rubber bands. Slip off the outside of the matchbox, slit it along one edge, and cut a bit off the length of the box (see the dotted line in the sketch). This outside part of the matchbox has to fit into the drawer section, breadthwise. Take a look at the shape on the right-hand side of the sketch: you fold the matchbox cover into a sort of triangle and stick it at the top. Then stick the triangle to the bottom of the drawer, at one end. Paint the whole thing and stretch some rubber bands over it. Now strum away merrily. (Look at the photograph on page 104: you will see the box in all its glory, bottom right).

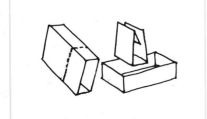

To make the *maraca* rattles which you can see in the sketch on the right you will need time and patience. You will need two balloons, the wooden handles of two old paint brushes (if your mother can spare them), newspapers, a sheet of plastic, wallpaper paste, poster-paint, paint brushes and varnish. Cover your work table with newspapers and have the plastic sheet ready. Make up the wallpaper paste. And now take a good look at the sketches:

1. Blow up the balloons and tie them tightly with string: be sure to leave an end hanging. From strong paper or card make a ring big enough to fit over the brush handle, and attach it with sticky tape over the mouths of the balloons.

2. Using the sharp edge of a ruler as a guide, tear up some newspapers into strips.

3. Lay the strips one by one on the plastic and paint them with wallpaper paste. Then put the strips on top of each other.

4. Wind the wet strips round the balloons, until you have built up two layers of paper. Be careful to leave the opening at the bottom free.

5. Leave the balloons to dry, in the oven if you like, about 200°F. (90°C.). (Gas mark ¼) .When they are completely dry, simply prick the balloons with a pin and pull them out of the hardened shells. Now pour some rice into the shells and fix the handles on with glue.

6. Wind a few more pasted strips round ball and joint.

7. Paint and varnish the *maracas*. Look at the photograph on page 104; your finished *maracas* are lying at the front on the left.

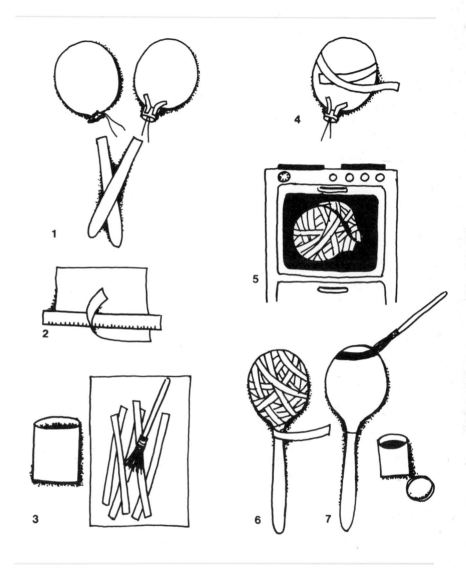

Making a tambourine is more complicated. Take one of those bases which are used for making baskets (obtainable in a craft shop) and paint and varnish it. A toy shop or craft shop should have the tinkling bells, which are tied with thin string to the holes in the base. Count the holes before you buy the bells so you will have enough. To the left in the photograph on page 104 you will see how pretty a tambourine like this can look.

A nice round tin—bottom side up—makes an ideal drum. But if you also want to make something really grand, you will first need to find a little wooden barrel. Other requirements: a good piece of chamois leather, cord, matches (wax if you can get them), a ring (which could be made of a double or triple coil of string), enamel paint, paint brush and paste.

Paint the drum: if you want to use several colours you must always wait until one colour is dry before applying the next, or they will run. When all the paint is thoroughly dry, cut the chamois into a circle about 1 in. (2 cm.) larger than the diameter of the drum. Then cut another strip ½ in. (1 cm.) wide from the remaining piece of chamois and glue it along the edge of the leather circle. In this reinforced edge you then pierce holes about 1 in. (2 cm.) apart, using a nail. Place the ring in the bottom of the barrel (as shown in drawing, top left) and fix the chamois circle over the end of the drum with cords run through the holes. Loop the cords over the ring on the inside of the barrel and, as in the drawing, insert matches into the cords and twist the cords round. Now the chamois leather is stretched like a real drum-skin! Take a good look at the drum opposite.

For the trumpet in the drawing, centre right, take a piece of fairly thin card and make a dunce's cap shape out of it. Stick it together with paste or sticky tape. Make a handle from some of the card left over and fix it to the trumpet. Now blow!

Something quite special—a *marimba* (an instrument you may have seen on television) made of bottles. (*See* third drawing on the right). Hang a number of empty beer bottles on a broomstick laid over two chairs. Pour some water into the bottles: the more water you put in, the higher the note you will get. Now strike the *marimba* chimes with a stick to your heart's content.

The instrument in the bottom sketch makes a surprising rattle. All you need are two empty plastic pots, which you fill with rice or dried peas. Join them together with sticky tape and rattle away.

Masks make the man

As far back as we know, men have made masks—to wear as actors, to frighten each other, or to celebrate. Think of a carnival, for instance. If you want to make your birthday party something completely different, make it a masked party. The masks can be as funny or as beautiful as you like. The diagram on page 108 shows you exactly how to begin. Using this pattern (we call it a 'template') you can make all the funny faces in the photograph opposite. Of course it's possible that if you follow our pattern exactly, the mask will turn out not to be the right size for your face or those of your friends. People's eyes, noses and mouths come in different positions and a mask like this must fit to some extent, so it is best to make a trial pattern first with an ordinary piece of paper and mark the position of your eyes, nose and mouth. Then cut out a piece of cardboard, using the test piece as a pattern, and once again mark where the eyes, etc. are to come. Snip out the nose so that it makes a cap over your own nose. The material you need is thin cardboard, on which you can paint or draw with a felt-tip pen. You can also cut out strips of coloured cardboard, or cardboard which you have painted yourself, and stick them on the masks. Hair and beard can be made of thick wool and stuck onto the mask. Make a hole on each side of the mask for a cord or piece of elastic to go around the head.

The photographs on the left illustrate how to make a mask out of a balloon. You will need newspapers, scissors, wallpaper paste, ordinary paste, poster-paint, water-paint, modelling wax, paint brushes, pencils, felt-tip pens, elastic and thread. And, of course, one or more balloons. Blow up the balloon and cover it with wallpaper paste. Stick on strips of newspaper which you have cut up beforehand. Build up several layers of paste and strips. Leave the balloon to dry (you can do this in the oven at about 200°F (90°C) (Gas mark ¼). Then cut the balloon in two halves: you now have two masks. You can model a nose from the wax. Stick it on the mask and paste newspaper strips over it. Leave it again to dry. Paint the mask, preferably twice over, with white poster-paint and give it its basic colour with another coat of paint. Now you can paint a face on the mask with a felt-tip pen or water-paint. Cut holes for the pupils of the eyes (then you can see through them) and stick on hair and beard. Make a hole for the elastic on each side of the mask.

Large template, left:
this is the pattern for
the masks on page 107.

Small template:
this is the pattern for
the eye-masks opposite.

Another possibility: masks made
from the paper carrier-bags your
mother uses for shopping. Never
use plastic bags, because you
won't be able to breathe! Put the
bag over your head and mark
where the eyes, nose and mouth
will come. You can cut holes in
these places. If the bag is too
long, cut some of it away. Or
you can make the long part into
a sort of fringe, snipped out as
shown in the centre sketch above.
Make as many variations as you
like: paint them with poster-
paint, or stick on coloured strips
of paper. Give the mask paper
ears, woolly hair and a beard,
like the pirate on page 107, bottom
right.

As you see, we have not taken our masks off yet; there are still more possibilities. You will find some on this page. If you want speed, these masks are the answer. They are much quicker and easier to make than the whole faces on the previous page, and if your party is tomorrow, you haven't much time...

To make the masquerade simpler, why not make half-masks? Have a good look at the 'small template' on page 108. Cut a half-mask out of white or coloured card. Paint it with poster-paint, or stick painted scraps of paper on it. You can also use brightly coloured felt-tip pens. If you want to be very grand, you can stick sequins or coloured beads on the masks. Study the sketches on this page: plenty of ideas here for funny, scary or really pretty masks.

A fancy-dress party

'Dressing up' is lots of fun. Somewhere in the house there is sure to be a box of old clothes, some pieces of material, or a discarded bedspread. Ask your mother if you can use any of the things you find, and then make your dream costume, hippy gear or comic outfit. If you do acting at school there may be a costume idea here for your teacher! Wigs, beards, masks and hats will complete the outfit of your choice; and you will find directions on how to make them on other pages of this book. Below we give instructions for making two of the costumes in the drawing. By following these you will be able to make the rest of the sweet or silly characters, as they are all made in the same way.

Two examples:
The hippy girl (below left, next to clown). First you make a hippy wig, as described on page 116. Then take an old sheet or bedspread to make a dress. Drape it round yourself, remembering to leave enough

material for a hem at the bottom. Now put a strong piece of elastic round your waist and mark the elastic to the size of your waist. Remove the elastic (making sure the marks remain in the proper place) and pin the skirt to the elastic, gathering the material as you do this. Stitch the elastic to the skirt. Turn up the hem, using big tacking stitches. Then cut out some flowers from an odd remnant of material and tack these onto the skirt. Now try on the wig and tie a band round it. Paint flowers on your cheeks with coloured felt-tip pens. You can turn yourself into a funny man with a big nose (third figure from the end below) with the help of a false nose, whiskers and an old hat with a flower pinned to it. (*See* page 118 for instructions on making the nose and whiskers, page 112 for the flower). Put on some funny glasses—you could remove the lenses from the frames— and pull an old jersey of your father's over your own clothes. You really *will* look like a comic character!

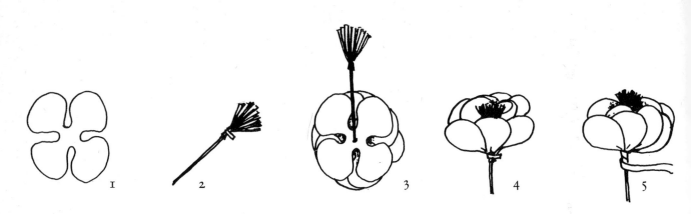

1   2   3   4   5

To make the 'poppy' which the funny little man on page 111 has on his hat, you will need 8 sheets of red tissue paper about 7 in. (18 cm.) square, and 1 sheet of black tissue paper 8 × 2½ in. (20 × 6 cm.); a strip of green crepe paper with the 'stretch' running lengthwise, a pipe cleaner, sticky tape and paste. Lay the 8 sheets of red tissue paper on top of each other and fold them into a square. Use the petal in the square below as a pattern. Place it in the folded corner of the square and cut around the edge. Unfold the petals (Sketch 1, above). Take the black tissue paper and cut a fringe along one edge of it. Roll the other edge round the pipe cleaner and fasten with sticky tape (Sketch 2). Make a hole in the centre of the four-sided petals and stick the pipe cleaner through the hole (Sketch 3). Turn the petals up all round it and tape them underneath (Sketch 4). Wind the strip of green crepe paper round the pipe cleaner and stick it down firmly (Sketch 5).

For the rose on the girl's mask on page 107 you need crepe paper (pink and green, for instance). Cut a piece of the pink crepe paper measuring 18 × 4 in. (40 × 10 cm.); fold the paper and wrap it round a pipe cleaner (Sketch 1, below right). Fasten with sticky tape and open out the rose. Cut four leaves from the green crepe paper (pattern left) and fix them under the rose (Sketch 2). Cut a long green strip of crepe paper with the stretch lengthwise and wind it round the pipe cleaner. Paste everything together firmly.

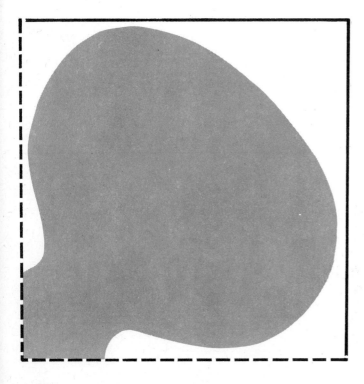

Funny hats

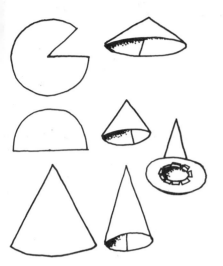

Hats—on your head, of course—are an essential part of any fancy-dress party. You could always use an old hat, but making one for yourself is really not too difficult, and much more fun. Take the witch's pointed hat, the clown's hat or the Chinese hat. These are the easiest to make, and you can adapt them endlessly. Have a look at the pattern on the left of this page. Take a thin sheet of card and cut out a circle, a semi-circle or a section of a circle, according to whether you want a flat, Chinese or pointed hat. Fold the card to a point as in the sketch and stick it together. For the witch's hat you must do a little more: snip round the bottom of the pointed hat at intervals, and cut out a brim to fit. Then bend back the little flaps you have made in the witch's hat and stick them firmly inside the brim. There!

Jewellery as a plaything

You need not be economical with the pretty ornaments in the photograph opposite, because you make them yourself—and of very cheap materials. When you are tired of them, pass them on to your little sister or brother to play with. They make very original and inexpensive presents!

The short necklace to the right of the photograph is made from the centre of a kitchen roll. Paint the cylinder—inside as well— with poster-paint and varnish it. Cut the cylinder in sections with a sharp, strong knife. If the pieces are slightly roughened by cutting, rub them with fine sandpaper and touch up with paint. String the rings on a coloured cord.

For the bracelets you need a tube used for posting calendars, etc., and you can get this in a stationery or office supply shop. Cut off sections of the tube with a sharp knife (you can cut all sorts of shapes, as shown in the photograph) and rub them down if necessary with fine sandpaper. Paint and varnish the bracelet; no end of colours and designs produce a splendid effect, so follow your fancy.

The long necklace in the middle of the photograph is made of kitchen-roll paper. The 'beads' are balls of paper covered with wallpaper paste. Leave the balls to dry (you can do this in an oven set at 200°F (90°C) (Gas mark $\frac{1}{4}$) and paint them (aniline dye is a good choice). Take a strong coloured cord, and using a big bodkin, thread it through your home-made beads.

You needn't envy this girl her fine jewels, because you can make them yourself— it's as easy as anything. Just read the directions on this page.

Wear a wig

Wigs are 'in' just now; your mother or your big sister may have one. Even grown-ups think it is fun to dress up and stop looking like themselves once in a while. Of course, little people don't need the kind of proper wig which looks like real hair. You can make really amusing ones from stockinet (your father may use it to clean the car, and you can buy it at most car accessory or hardware shops). Skeins of wool are very good, too.

In the sketches on the left of this page you can see different ways of making wigs. For instance, you can make a sort of cap from an old nylon stocking or half a pair of tights (sketch 1). Gather the cut-off section at the top and tie a thread round it. Or of course you could use an old hat without the brim as a base for your wig. Now look at sketch 2: sew little scraps of wool or stockinet to the cap or hat. If you put it over an upturned basin while you do the work you will avoid puckering and making the cap too small. When your wig is as thick as you want, dye it with stocking or clothes dye, which you can buy at the chemist's. Just dip the whole wig into the dye-bath.

In sketch 4 you can see a pretty, long-haired wig. You get the effect by using very long strands of wool, so this wig is not specially difficult to make.

The simplest wig of all is made by plaiting skeins of wool and stitching them onto a nice handkerchief or scarf, as in sketch 5 (don't forget the fringe!) Knot the scarf under your chin and the effect is terrific!

A false nose and a false beard

You can make a colossal nose like the one in the photograph on the left with an empty toilet roll. If this is too long unroll part of it before you begin to make your nose. Over the roll you stick strips of newspaper which you have covered with wallpaper paste. When the nose is dry, paint it with poster-paint and varnish it. Make holes on either side of the roll to attach string or elastic to tie around your head. The round nose in the photograph opposite is made in the same way, but with something round as a base instead of a toilet roll. For instance, you could use a ball or small bowl.

You can make this delightful disguise set with stockinet or skeins of knitting wool. When you have carefully shaped and clipped the eyebrows, moustache and beard you can sew them onto plasters; then stick the plasters to your face. Or use double-sided sticky tape: simply stick the hair on one side and press the other side to your face. Add a pair of sunglasses and not a living soul will recognize you!

Make yourself a jigsaw puzzle

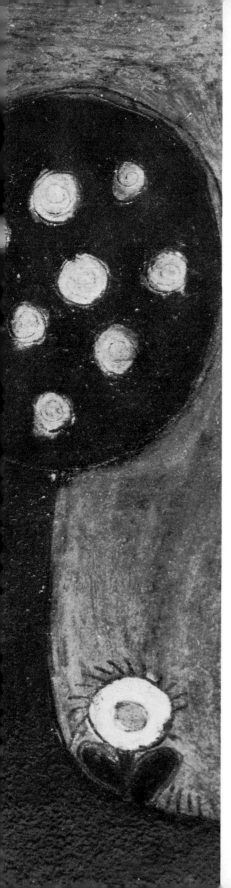

You can buy puzzles of every shape and colour, but why not make one yourself? You are sure to have a beautiful picture you could use for this, or one you have painted yourself. This is a splendid idea when you want to give a birthday present.

A piece of cardboard will be best for your homemade puzzle—the back of a good note pad would do very well. Make your drawing on the cardboard and colour it with water-colours or pastel crayons. Then coat the picture with a clear varnish (remember, if you have used watercolours, to wait until the paint is completely dry). Let the varnish dry before cutting the cardboard in small pieces with a knife or strong scissors.

If you want your homemade puzzle as a treat for a very small sister or brother, it must not be too complicated. In this case, cut out each object in the picture separately. Very small children will find it quite difficult enough just putting the picture together again!

If you want to make the puzzle very quickly because it is some-one's birthday tomorrow, here is another idea. Find an old picture postcard or calendar and glue it to the cardboard. Then cut-out the puzzle. If you want to make an extra-difficult puzzle for

someone who can put even a very complicated jigsaw together in a moment, use two picture post-cards or calendars (or your homemade drawings, of course). You can be sure that even the brightest 'puzzler' won't succeed immediately—and you will have a good laugh…

Artistic patchwork

Patchwork has always been the art of combination. This artistic and now traditional craft came into being a couple of hundred years ago. At that time patchwork was based on the concept of 'thrift and industry' which gave women the bright idea of using up the remnants and scraps of material to the last centimetre by working them into a patchwork quilt. In pioneering days in America, thrift was so important that housewives could not afford to waste any scraps of material which were still usable. Cloth was expensive and hard to come by for women in the New World, but they were

That there is real art concealed in the ragbag is proved by this coverlet. It is composed of rectangles carefully arranged to give a light and dark 'rhythm'. Opposite you can see an enlarged section of the patchwork. A superficial glance gives the impression that all the squares are made up of the same materials. Nothing could be further from the truth. The strips appear similar, but they are cut out of dozens of different remnants. If you look closely at the detail, you will see very small lines of stitches, which show that this one was hand-sewn in the genuine old-fashioned way. If you prefer to use a machine, the result will not suffer at all.

thrifty and econom and from this combination patchwork was born. Gradually the importance of colour and design was incorporated into patchwork. Complicated patterns were worked out, the patches laid side by side and sewn into dazzling covers, cushions, hangings and other upholstery for the home. All this took time, a long time in fact, and woman would spend many months working on a quilt. In those days people, unlike ourselves, were quite used to the idea that such things took time. Don't be scared off by this 'long story'; after all, we have our sewing machines…

Interest in patchwork has recently revived in England and America, Sweden and the Netherlands, with the result that a traditional craft has been adapted to contemporary interiors. The photographs on the following pages show patchwork in a modern house, a cheerful encounter between yesterday and today. See how modern the patchwork looks. You need not take a great deal of trouble over this—the scraps of material you will be using will be contemporary enough to make a cushion cover, quilt, or wall panel seem very up-to-date. When you have your first try at patchworking, you might make something in a more traditional style, where simplicity of design is the distinguishing feature. Your piece of work may be a cushion cover, or, if you want to start big, a real patchwork quilt. From the scraps of material you have (and you must take a good look at all your remnants to see if they are useful), you cut equal-sized squares. First sew these squares together in long strips—you can do it on the sewing machine—and then sew the strips together widthwise. This is the quick way to make a quilt. After you have finished sewing the strips together, back them with a lining, and put the spread on your bed. If you have children, it may be difficult to keep the bedspread for yourself, because they know how 'in' patchwork is.

All you can do is make another. When your own ragbag is empty, the whole family can go collecting from friends and acquaintances and this will get you quite a lot further. Your first bit of patch-working need not be in a traditional style. There are no 'must's' at all when you are working with patches—it is up to you to see what can be done with them. If you want to be really true to tradition, let the ragbag decide. A patchwork made entirely from old scraps will resemble those made by your great grandmothers. It is good sport making new things from old, and fun to see in your cushion cover a scrap of a favourite summer dress or a remnant from a shirt once worn by someone you like.

In general no background is needed for patchwork, but in this modern design one was used. The result is original and contemporary. The motifs from which the pattern is built up are identical in shape and fit together exactly.

Patchwork in practice

Naturally some materials are much nicer to work with than others. Calico, for instance, is often preferred because it is so easy to handle. It is easy to wash, too, which may be very necessary with some articles. Silk gives beautiful effects but it has a tendency to fray. Old cravats have less of this tendency, and are also easier to work with. Woollen materials are difficult to sew and not at all easy to keep clean. Steaming may be a solution with a woollen patchwork, as long as the materials are not so different in texture (and they may be) that even steaming is ineffective. Remember that whatever material you choose, the scraps for one piece of work must be similar as regards the cleaning method they need. If you use fabrics which call for very different handling, the finished work will be difficult to clean, because one section may tend to run, another to shrink, etc. If you want to go still further in the art of combination, there is the possibility of plunging all the different scraps of material you are going to use into a dye-bath. Each scrap—even if it has no design—will take up the dye in its own way; and this will result in a subtle liveliness of tone. In this way you could make a coverlet in richly chequered shades of red, blue, green, or what you will.

Patience for a thing of beauty
The detailed photograph of the patchwork on p. 123, showing how the pattern was constructed, is worth a second look. A quilt like this one is not sewn in an evening. It requires time and patience in the old style to make a thing of beauty. The pattern consists of dozens of squares built up ingeniously from scraps of material. The material was laid strip by strip on a backing and then sewn by hand (you could do it by machine too). The pattern was worked from the centre outwards. When the (green) square was in place, the design was built up with strips which were first sewn wrong side out in the desired position and then folded over. By ironing each strip in place the result is kept wrinkle-free.

With this method no stitches can be seen, while each new strip holds the previous one in position. Through this whole procedure the patches were stitched straight onto the lining, which gave them extra strength. There is art in your ragbag, so start picking out scraps.

The baby-seat and the bedspread on the right are made in the pioneer style, while the wall hanging is a more complex design, involving an appliqué technique. The swinging baby-seat was lined with a tough material, and the gaps for the toddler's legs were bound with a tough, but not rough, material. The bedspread was also lined, for strength and to guard against fraying.

These cushions look surprisingly modern, even though the designs are the traditional ones used in the early days of patchworking. They provide the best proof that good patchwork does not age, If you want to make something traditional, you can get some ideas from these cushion covers.

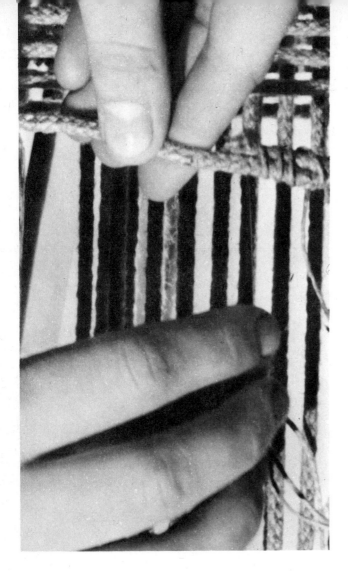

The days of the old chairmender are long past, but this does not mean that you yourself cannot get weaving with excellent results. These two pages show how simple it is. For this job get yourself some flax twine of about ¼ in. (4 mm.) thickness (usually obtainable from a ship-chandler in rolls of about 100 yards (60 m.)). If you cannot find any, buy ¼ in. (4 mm.) nylon cord, but note that nylon tends to attract dirt and dust. The transverse line in the seat of the chair (below) is one-third the seat-depth, measured from the back of the seat.

Start by weaving the transverse cords, taking two turns round the bar before stretching the cord across to the opposite bar. Pull the cord as tight as possible and make sure that the strands are jammed tightly together. Sew the end to the final double-turn on the underside of the seat. Mark where the change in pattern is to come in the lengthwise weaving. This design is not only decorative but it makes the chair particularly comfortable to sit on.

Weave lengthwise as follows: turn the chair upside down and sew the end of the cord on firmly with very thin string or wire, beginning on the right. With the chair right side up again, bring the cord over the transverse web as far as the mark (see opposite page). Then pass it under the transverse cords, back to the back bar. From the back bar the cord is passed over the top of the seat to the marked line, and then under the transverse cords to the front bar. Take a double turn round the front bar before passing the end back over the seat again. Be careful to keep your starting and finishing off on the underside of the seat.

Simple sofa cushions

Thanks to the cushions, the seats on these pages look quite exceptional. You can very easily make these cushions yourself. The basic material is foam rubber.

Box sofa
Foam rubber is obtainable in different consistencies. It is advisable to use a harder type for the seat than for the back. Buy the foam in the size, consistency and thickness required and have it cut to size in the shop. Use the working drawing on page 132 as the basic pattern for cutting out the cushion cover. Cut out two identical pieces for the seat and backrest and allow for a $\frac{3}{4}$ in. (1.5 cm.) seam on each side.

Chests where you keep odds and ends which are not in constant use can do sterling service as seats or guest beds if they are covered with thick, comfortable cushions. The headrest slung in loops the full length of the seat is unusually effective.

Leave ¾ in. (1.5 cm.) for the side seams as well. Sew the sides together first, then sew the top onto them, then the bottom. Leave plenty of space to insert the foam rubber. When you have properly stuffed the cushions, hemstitch the opening by hand. The headrest slung in loops above the sofa is not only decorative and comfortable but prevents greasy patches on the wall. You can stuff this with synthetic materials, kapok, old nylons, down or scraps of material. Since the headrest has no sides the front of the covering can be sewn directly to the back. However, it is wise to give the covering an underslip, so that it can easily be removed for washing. For the loops, which hang from copper rings, you can buy a heavy piece of tape or make a piece from the scraps of material.

A simple bench seat can look quite different if some original backrests are hung on the wall above it. The materials needed are simple and they are not difficult to make. Make two backrests, leaving a space of a few centimetres between them.

You can easily cut out the cushions with the help of this pattern. One possibility for the wall fixture is to use screws with matching caps (obtainable in various colours) which can be popped over the head of the screw. Drill holes in the wall and plug them first.

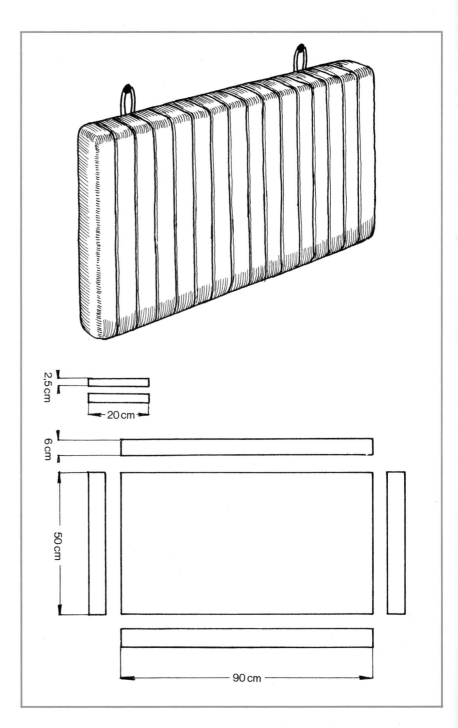

2.5 cm

←20 cm→

6 cm

50 cm

←————— 90 cm —————→

Make sure that the copper rings—also available from a ship-chandler —are securely screwed to the wall (with plugs!) before hanging up the headrest.

Backrests with loops
The cushion in the sketch opposite measures $35\frac{1}{2} \times 19\frac{1}{2}$ in. (90 × 50 cm.) and the foam rubber is $2\frac{1}{2}$ in. (6 cm.) thick. Cut your material according to the pattern; double the material, cut out front and back. If two cushions are being made, the four side pieces can also be cut double. Leave a $\frac{3}{4}$ in. (1.5 cm.) margin on all sides for the seams. Sew the side seams first, then the top and lastly the bottom. Make sure that you leave one edge open, underneath at the back. Hemstitch this by hand after you have put in the foam rubber. Cut the loops according to the pattern 1 in. (2.5 cm.) wide, but without an extra $\frac{3}{4}$ in. (1.5 cm.) for the seam. Fold the strip of material in two lengthwise and stitch together along the long edge. Turn the strip inside out and press under a damp cloth. Sew the loops to the back of the cushions. Secure to the wall with the help of plugs, copper-coloured cuphooks or screws with loose caps which can be fitted over them. Be sure to allow enough space between to keep the backrest clear of the seat when in position.

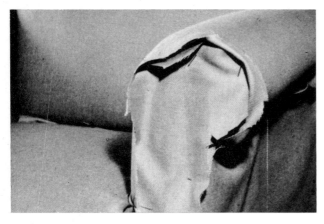

Leave generous seam allowances of 1 in. (2.5 cm.) so that you can make adjustments and correct any mistakes.
Curved pins are a help if you are working with thick materials. This sort of pin is particularly advisable if you are using piping.

It is of the greatest importance that the fabric grain should run straight in each section. Check this while you are pinning the various parts on the chair.
When you are certain that everything fits properly, fold back the seams and chalk along the pinned seam lines to guide your sewing along them.

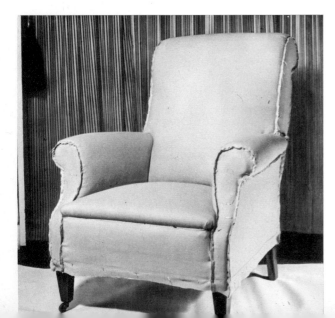

Making a chair slipcover is a precision job which demands time and care. The first requirement is not great experience of sewing, but patience. If you follow the instructions for chair covering described on these pages point by point, you will soon see see that it is not as difficult as it looks at first sight also that it can be a very pleasant and satisfying job. Leave the old upholstery on. The new cover is designed for removal in one piece for easy cleaning.

Working out the quantity of material
Suitable fabrics are woven cretonnes, which may be combined with linen, or a woollen material combined with synthetic fibres. Above all, the material must be crease-proof and stretch-proof. It is safer to choose a plain fabric or one with a small, simple pattern; and if you are a beginner, big patterns are out.
Most furnishing fabrics are obtainable in widths of 48–50 in. (120–130 cm.). Draw on paper a long strip 5 in. (12–13 cm.) wide. Now measure up all the parts of the chair with the tape measure and add 1 in. (2.5 cm.) extra for the seams along all the edges. You will need an extra 5 in. (12.5 cm.) to tuck in along the sides of the seat. Also add this amount to all those parts which will have to be tucked round the edge of the seat. Draw the measured parts on paper in the scale of 1:12 (1:10); cut out the measured parts and lay them along the long 5 in. (12–13 cm.) strip which you have drawn. Multiply by 12 (10) and you will then know how much material you will need. Remember that the grain of the fabric should be straight on all parts of the chair. If you are using a patterned fabric, make sure that the pattern matches up on the different parts of the chair. It is advisable to pin the material right side up on the chair. Now we can start.
1. Begin with the material on the front of the seat back. Pin the fabric to the chair from top to bottom

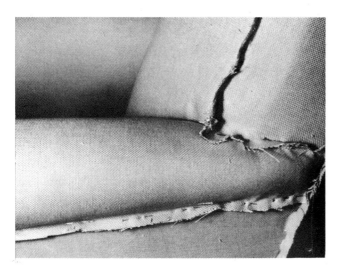

This photograph shows that the armrest fabric is tucked into the join at the back. Another possibility is to sew this to the back. The method is described in the text.

down the centre of the back, then along all the sides. Leave a 1 in. (2.5 cm,) allowance for the seams and 5 in. (12.5 cm.) for tucking down the edges of the seat.

Where necessary cut notches in the seam which comes over the top of the chair arm, but make them no more than ½ in. (1 cm.) deep.

2. For the seat allow 5 in. (12.5 cm.) extra at the back and along the sides for tucking the material down along the edges. Lay the material flat over the seat and pin outwards from the middle, then along the sides. Depending on the shape of the chair, pin the material for the front panel from the top downwards.

3. For the back, once again pin from the middle outwards, then along the edges, allowing a seam of 1 in. (2.5 cm.) and 2 in. (5 cm.) extra at the bottom (to be secured under the seat of the chair with adhesive tape).

4. Sides of the chairback, above the armrest: pin to the seam lines of the front and back of the chairback cover. Leave a seam of 1 in. (2.5 cm.) all round.

5. The fronts of the armrests. (Are you constantly checking that the material is lying snug and the fabric grain running straight?) Pin from the middle outwards, then the seam lines along the edges, allowing 1 in. (2.5 cm.) for the seams. With old chairs you may find that the arms are no longer identical in shape, so that the material has to be pinned on both fronts. As a rule, one front section can be taken off and used as a pattern for the second section, making sure that the design matches up, if you are using a patterned material.

6. The inside of the armrests: first make sure that the fabric grain runs from front to back, or if the fabric has a pattern that this shows on the top of the armrest. Work from the middle outwards, pin the seam line to the front edge and allow for a 1 in. (2.5 cm.) seam. Now pin the edge of the armrest to the backrest of the chair, again allowing for the seam. Leave 5 in. (12.5 cm.) for tucking in round the seat. Make notches along the rounded seam edges—not deeper than ½ in. (1 cm.)—in order to ease the fabric and avoid wrinkles. Take this section off the chair and use it as a pattern for cutting out the other armrest.

7. The outside panels of the armrests, where the fabric grain must run from top to bottom: pin from the middle outwards, making sure that the fabric just under the armrests falls smoothly. Pin along the edges, allowing 1 in. (2.5 cm.) for the seams and an additional 2 in. (5 cm.) at the bottom, to be secured underneath the seat with adhesive tape. If you want to sew a hem along the base, keep a 1 in. (2.5 cm.) allowance at the bottom.

Now pin all the seams together on the chair, checking that all the fabric is fitting smoothly and snugly. The wide seam allowances leave room

for adjustments where necessary. When everything is properly fitted, trim back the seam allowances to $\frac{1}{2}$ in. (1 cm.) (or you can do this after sewing), except for the right-hand seam on the back of the chair, where the zip fastener should be. With the cover still on the chair, mark along the pinline of the seams (that is, on the wrong side of the fabric) with tailor's chalk. Every $2\frac{1}{2}$ in. (6 cm.) make a different mark, such as a circle or a dash at right angles to the seam. These marks will be a great help to you when you come to match up the seams before sewing them.

If the chair is to be finished off with a ground-length hem, the upholstery can be secured underneath the seat with adhesive tape.

The hem can be straight or gathered. If you prefer a straight hem, set a box-pleat in each corner as shown in the photograph.

Another possibility is to start the zip from the top of the hem and close the hem with a press stud in the box-pleat in the back right-hand corner.

If in spite of careful fitting and measuring, the sides of the seat will not stay tucked in, make some tube-like bolsters and stuff these down inside the crevices.

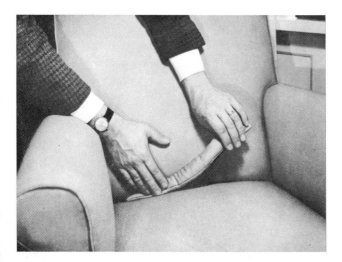

Finishing touches

Your chair will look particularly well finished if piping is sewn along the seams that show. To make piping, cover long pieces of cord, with bias strips of fabric. Fold a bias strip over a length of cord and sew the fabric together as close as possible to the cord—that's your piping. Then tack it on to the right side of the fabric, with the stitch line of the piping on the chalked line of the fabric and sew together. Place the second piece of fabric over the stitched part with the piping, making sure that the right sides of the fabric are together. Tack the whole thing neatly before sewing.

While tacking and sewing, make sure that the marks along the seams match up. Work section by section, and after tacking, check to see that each section of the cover fits correctly before you sew it to another section. Begin with the back sections, then tack, fit and sew the side edges above the armrests to the back sections. Next tack and sew the armrests (inserting the piping as you go), and add the fronts of the armrests to the inside and outside edges of the armrest sections. Fit before stitching, and tack all of this to the back section. Stitch the seat in last. When you come to inserting the zip, make sure that it is long enough to reach from the bottom of the cover to a point above the armrest. The zip opening should of course be at the bottom of the cover. If you are going to make a hem round the bottom of the cover, the zip can be fitted into it when you have turned up the hem. Keep the hem $\frac{3}{4}$ in. (2 cm.) clear of the floor and tailor a box-pleat at each corner. The bottom end of the zip fastener should begin in the box-pleat in the back right-hand corner of the hem. Sew piping in where the zip is inserted.

Something to embroider

Relying on only a few elementary principles, which seem to be little more than common sense, you can do almost anything you like with embroidery. Whether you want to keep to the clear guide of a pattern, to design one for yourself, or to embroider at random, you will find the instructions set down on these pages a very helpful guide.

The illustrations on the following pages of this chapter show that it is possible to do embroidery in a great variety of ways. The game has scarcely any rules. In addition to the creative one, there is a practical side to embroidery. The choice of materials, for instance, is partly a matter of practical considerations. Decide whether the finished piece for work is to be washed or dry cleaned and select your materials accordingly. A wall-hanging may not need to be washed, but placemats

Any of the sixteen different fabrics shown below can be used for embroidery. Remember to over-cast raw edges of material to prevent fraying, ravelling and general annoyance.

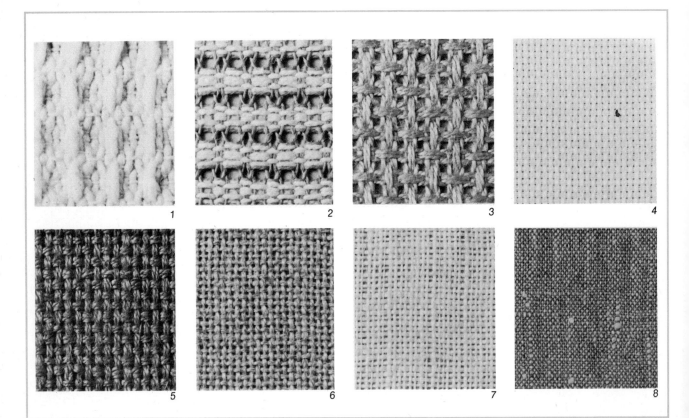

and tablecloths inevitably land up in the suds. Remember, too,
that both the background and the thread you use will affect the
character of your piece of embroidery.

Take a close look at the illustrations of the sixteen different fabrics
which you can use as a basis for embroidery or appliqué work. If you
haven't got a real 'feeling' for materials, ask someone who understands
them to tell you more about the suitability of the illustrated textiles.
1) Waffle weave; 2) 'rya' weave; 3 and 4) leno weaves; 5) 'binca' (jute)
weave; 6) hopsack; 7) linen; 8) Union (cannot be numbered off, therefore
unsuitable for cross-stitch patterns); 9) wool or dralon; 10) felt;
11–15) various linens (numbers 11 and 12 cannot be numbered off);
16) interfacing.

Embroidery tools consist of a series of needles, large cutting-out

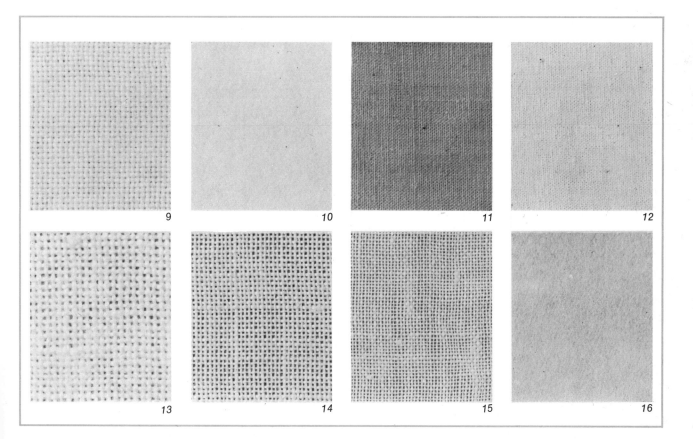

scissors, small pointed scissors and a thimble for that middle finger which can get pricked so often. As for needles, experience will teach you when to use a short one and when a long. The thickness of the needle depends on the thread you use—it should pass easily through the eye of the needle. And for a loosely woven fabric you use a blunt needle, for a finer weave a sharp one.

Let's take a look at the sketch showing the method of holding the thread in place without a knot. When you start your embroidery, insert the needle and thread on the right side (a) and let the end of the thread hang down until the first stitches have been made. Then stitch the thread back again (b) and loop it among the stitches on the back. If you are using a flat embroidery stitch, such as satin stitch, you can secure the thread by using small tacking stitches (c) which will later be covered and held by the embroidery stitch. On each subsequent start and finish, pass the thread through the stitches on the back. Never knot the thread; when you press the work the knots inevitably appear in the form of bumps on the front of the work.

Embroidery work should be pressed carefully on the back, under a slightly damp, preferably cotton cloth, such as a tea towel. Make sure there is no starch in the pressing cloth. To avoid creasing the embroidery, lay it on a soft base, a thin sheet of foam rubber or plastic foam, covered with cotton or a piece of blanket. Or make a special flat pressing base from a piece of cotton laid over layers of cotton wool. After pressing, remove the pressing cloth and iron the work—on the wrong side—with a medium-hot iron.

Below: securing the first thread.

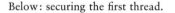

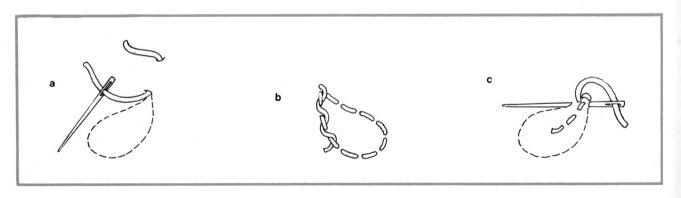

Right: needles, scissors, and thimble. See that you always have them by you. And don't go cutting paper with the scissors, it blunts them!

Below: wool, silk and cotton embroidery yarns, a wide choice of colours and textures.

Scenes from the ragbag

Some browsing through the ragbag should supply an inspiring pile of oddments and snippets for appliqué work—figures cut out of material —which you sew on a background by hand or with the sewing machine. Appliqués are generally used for wall panels and tablecloths, but it is not difficult to think of other objects to which an 'animal-vegetable-mineral' decoration like the one opposite could be applied. The secret of beautiful appliqué work lies in its simplicity, as it is difficult to sew on complicated motifs which have too many corners. It is also practical to apply a very fine iron-on interfacing to the back of the appliqué, to prevent the fabric from fraying and make it easier to sew.

The drawings below show how the round cloth opposite was made. (a) Measure out a circle and pin round it. Then tack round it and remove the pins. (b) The next step is to iron the interfacing on to the pieces to be used for the appliqué. Draw the figures on the white interfacing, remembering that they will appear mirror-wise when fixed to the background. (c) Experiment with placing the figures in different positions on the background. A whole family worked on this cloth! When you are pleased with your arrangement, pin the figures to the background and then tack them in place. Use a blanket or herringbone stitch to sew the figures to the background. Details such as eyes, noses and mouths can be added later with a 'free' embroidery stitch.

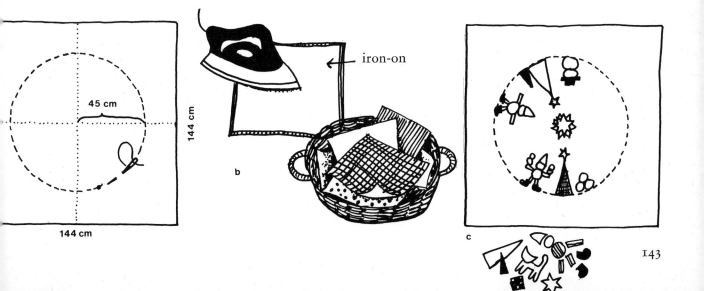

iron-on

45 cm

144 cm

144 cm

b

c

The drawings on this page show how patterns can be transferred with a fine, transparent iron-on interfacing. The method is as follows: (a) Lay the interfacing, adhesive side up, on the pattern and trace the outline of the drawing with a soft pencil. Then reverse the interfacing

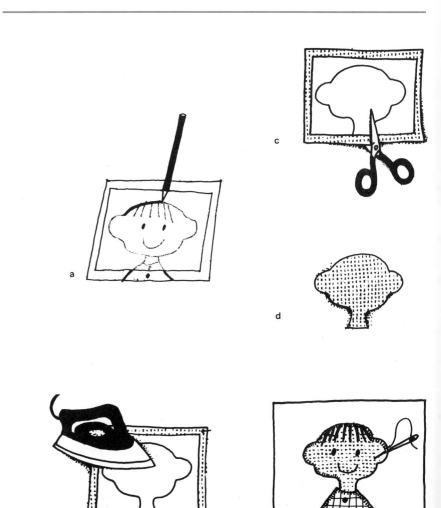

and copy the outline of the pattern on this side as well. (b) Now iron the interfacing on the back of the fabric and (c) cut out the figure. (d) In this case the result will not be a mirror image. If you want to see results very quickly, you can resort to double-sided iron-on interfacing.

Another form of appliqué work is shown in the construction of this little creature: (f) interfacing patterns are ironed on to the fabric, leaving a hem of about ½ in. (1 cm.) notched as in (g). (h) Turn in the hem and tack it. (i) Tack the figure to the background and secure with invisible hemstitching. One the right you can see various ways of securing appliqué. You know them already; (j) hemstitch, (k) blanket stitch, (l) herringbone, (m) machine zig-zag and (n) a free stitch which you can invent yourself, to give the effect of hair or tufts of feathers, for instance.

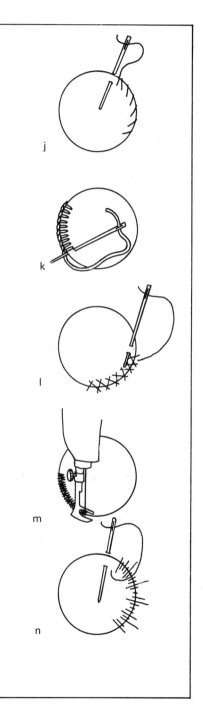

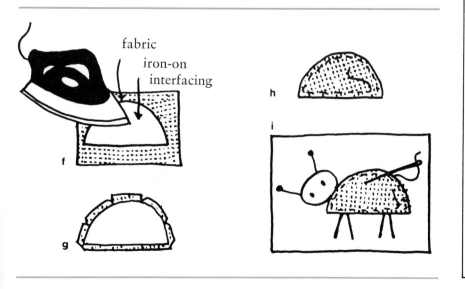

Detail of a cushion cover: the houses are outlined in back stitch and filled in with stem stitch, chain stitch, bullion and blanket stitch, with a French knot here and there.

If you are going for colour, this flower motif, suitable for a cushion cover or other purposes, allows you to work in a great variety of colours. No pattern here; just imagination and a bit of enterprise to guide you. **More about houses and flowers on pages 148 and 149.**

Copying allowed

If you have the courage to draw a pattern freehand on a piece of material, use a sharp pencil, or for a coarse fabric, a ball-point. With carbon paper (which is obtainable in several colours) it is easier still: pin the pattern to the material along the top and left-hand edges, insert the carbon paper and trace over the outline with a pencil or ball-point. 'See-through' materials can simply be placed on top of the pattern and the outlines traced. You can also use a prick-out pattern, made of tough drawing paper: place the sheet with the pattern on a soft background and prick holes at equal distances along the pattern lines with a darning needle. You could also do the pricking with a sewing machine, using the unthreaded needle to do the pricking. Smooth off any roughness on the back with fine emery paper. Place the fabric on which you will draw the pattern against a smooth background and lay the pricked pattern on top, with a weight at each corner to prevent slipping. Dip your finger, a brush or a wodge of cottonwool in the oil paint—which may be slightly diluted with petroleum—and rub the paint through the holes. Use dark paint on a light fabric and white paint on

(a) Transferring a pattern with carbon paper. As far as possible avoid moving the paper about, as it will make marks. They can be washed out, of course, but not all fabrics will be amenable to this treatment. (b and c) If you want to dilute the artist's oil paints used for prick-out patterns with turpentine, go slowly, because if the paint is too thin it will seep into the material.

a dark fabric. After marking, leave the material to dry thoroughly, and clean the pattern if you want to use it again.

Transferring a pattern is not difficult, but designing a pattern yourself is easier still. An embroidery pattern need not be complicated—a simple idea will be effective if you use imaginative combinations of colours and materials. Look at the drawings of the little boy and the houses (on page 148). Though dull at first, the drawings change as spots, stripes, squares, flowers and stars are added. Anything you fancy can be tried out first on paper and then transferred to the material. But let's suppose that you want to avoid making patterns. Experiment with different colours and try making every stitch you know or can dream up. Look at the photograph on page 147. You can make your design as varied as you wish—there's usually space for another little star or a French knot even in the smallest corner.

Left: You could copy the idea of the little boy and his dog. For the block of houses, take a look at the ones in colour on page 146.

Below: This is how your experiment begins, when you set out to embroider without a pattern. You can 'plant' the first flower anywhere you like, as long as it is in balance. The rest follows naturally. But who says you have to have flowers? You could just as well have people! (right-hand bottom corner).

This cheerful woolly
⟨fell⟩oo is made of pom-
⟨p⟩oms. You probably
⟨k⟩now how to make
⟨th⟩em; but if not,
⟨ta⟩ke a look at page
⟨15⟩2.

Would you believe
⟨th⟩at an eight-year-
⟨o⟩ld designed this
⟨pi⟩rate? On page 153
⟨y⟩ou can follow how
⟨h⟩e sewed the bold
⟨r⟩ascal together.

The pompoms

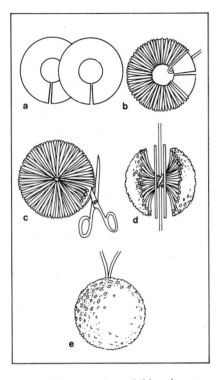

You only have to show children how to do this once and for the rest of the rainy afternoon they will be able to make pompoms from all sorts of snippets of wool. They can make animals from pompoms or tie clusters of pompoms together as a playful decoration for the nursery.

To make pompoms, follow the drawing on the left: a) cut out two circles of cardboard, with a hole in the centre, of the size you want for the pompoms; b) hold the circles together and wind wool through them, as thickly and evenly as you can; c) when you have closed up the centre, insert the point of your scissors between the rings and cut the pompom open round the edge; d) Tie a double thread tightly round the middle of the pompom, slit the cardboard rings and remove them. Leave the ends of the centre thread hanging; you can use them to tie the pompoms together. e) Shake the pompom out into a pretty ball, and hold it over a steaming kettle for a minute or two.

Animals ball by ball
For an owl you need two pompoms tied firmly together. Eyes and beak are cut out of felt or thick paper and glued on. The little owl stands on wire claws bound with wool. The rabbits are also made by tying two pompoms together. Add a tiny pompom in the right place for the tail. The handsome ears consist of two layers of felt, sewn together with tiny overstitching. The eyes are also made of white felt and can be given different expressions with a felt-tip pen. The teeth are made of paper, glued on with a fabric adhesive. The head of Leo the Lion is a pompom made up of half dark and half light yellow wool. After cutting the pompoms open, the dark part is clipped into a 'face', leaving the light wool as a mane. Leo's nose is an orange pompom and he looks out from black felt eyes (these parts having been stuck on with a fabric glue). The body is a light yellow pompom, and the tail is a plait of wool with a tuft at the end.

One large and one small pompom go to make up the parrot. He comes out in stripes because the cardboard rings have had a layer of white wool wound round them first, then a layer of dark purple, then light purple, then violet, and finally a layer of white. When you slit the rings the smart stripes appear. Beak and eyes are made of felt. The beak is cut double, sewn together with overstitching, and then stuffed with cotton wool. Beak and eyes are attached with glue, as is the parrot's tail. He hangs on to his perch with claws made of pipecleaners wrapped in wool.

Small hands can show amazing skill in making things, even though we may have to help a bit if a lot of patience is needed. For young children who want to get on with the work, suggest that they try making a wall-hanging like the one on page 151. The eight-year-old who designed this pirate made his own drawing first and used his mother's sewing machine to do the zig-zag stitching. If you don't trust a child with your machine, let him appliqué the design with firm tacking and 'free' stitches. This is how the pirate was made. First the boy traced the various parts of the pirate on to iron-on interfacing, then he ironed them on to coloured materials and cut them out. The red circle was tacked on to the backing before the other parts of the body and the clothes were put in position. Using his mother's sewing machine, the boy appliquéd the pieces with a zig-zag stitch, varying the width of the stitch and using different coloured threads. Hair and beard were made by zig-zagging to and fro a number of times. The only things glued on were the black felt buttons. When he finished sewing, the boy's mother lined the wall-hanging for him.

Do your children sometimes bring home terrific drawings like this one? Perhaps you can encourage them to give drawings greater permanence in fabric, if you yourself are not keen to reproduce them.

Jolly mini-cakes

No cake is just like another—that is obvious from the works of art you see illustrated here. Of course they may be created by the housewife, but why shouldn't husband and children have a go at the weekend? All the little cakes in the photograph were made by children.

Buy plain sponge cakes and prepare the butter cream to garnish the cakes in advance. The ingredients you need are:

½ pint (3 decilitres) milk
1 egg or 2 egg yolks
1 tablespoon sugar
1 teaspoon plain or potato flour
½ teaspoon vanilla sugar
3½ oz. (100 g.) butter
2½ oz. (75 g.) caster sugar

Mix the egg or yolks, sugar and flour thoroughly. Heat the milk and add it, stirring all the time. Transfer the mixture to a saucepan and bring to the boil, beating it to a thick yellow consistency. Then quickly transfer the mixture to a bowl and add the vanilla sugar. Mix 3½ oz. (100 g.) butter and 2½ oz (75 g.) caster sugar until they are soft and creamy, and add this little by little to the cooked mixture, stirring gently. Then you are ready to make the icing for the artistic cakes.

You will need:
5 oz. (150 g.) icing sugar
1 white of egg
1 teaspoon lemon juice

Beat the ingredients together until smooth. Then divide the mixture into several cups and add different colours (obtainable from the grocer). Cocoa, coffee and red jam will do just as well, though your colour range will then be restricted to dark and light brown and bright red. Now you can let your husband and children have a go. The coloured icing should be spread on the cakes with a knife. If different colours are to be applied over or alongside each other, it is best to wait until each layer of icing is dry to prevent the colours from running. When the cakes are iced, put on the butter cream. You could also colour the cream with food colours, put it in a plastic piping bag, and let your family pipe out attractive shapes. For further decoration chocolate buttons are excellent, and of course, whipped cream.

Gingerbread magic

The whole family can be creative when it comes to making old-fashioned gingerbread cookies. With a little bit of talent you can set your hand to making dogs, flowers, little people, a train, a house or even a whole gingerbread castle. Here is a basic recipe for ginger cookies; of course you can vary the quantities to your liking.

You will need:
14 oz. (400 g.) brown sugar
¾ pt. (4½ dl.) milk or cream
5–6 oz. (150–175 g.) butter or margarine
2 tablespoons (½ dl.) honey and 2 tablespoons (½ dl.) treacle
1½ tablespoons cinnamon
1½ tablespoons ginger
1½ lb. (750 g.) self-raising flour

Stir the sugar, honey and treacle, the spices and milk or cream in a saucepan over low heat to a fluid consistency. Leave to cool. Then mix in the flour and knead everything into a stiff dough. Put the dough in a cool place to chill before rolling it on a board to a thickness of about an ¼ in. (4 mm.). Then with a sharp knife cut out the various parts of the cookie shapes you want to make. Do this on a greased baking tray, and leave the cookies on the tray so they will hold their shape. Put the baking tray in a moderate oven (about 376°F) (190°C) (Gas mark 4) for 15 to 30 minutes. Allow the cookies to cool before lifting them off the tray.

Flat biscuit shapes—such as flowers, houses, animals and trees—are the easiest to make. Roll out the dough and cut out the figures—inspiration will come naturally while you work. If you want to be precise about the figures you make, draw them first on greaseproof paper. Cut out the patterns and place them on the dough. Then you can cut the figure out neatly along the outlines of your pattern. If you plan to make a family occasion of it, and build the castle pictured here, turn to the next page where you will find a description of three-dimensional ginger cookies.

Decorate your creations with icing. Beat —the quantities naturally depend on the size of the edifice—10 oz. (300 g.) icing sugar and 2 egg whites to a firm consistency, Colour with food colouring; if you want to use several colours, it is best to use different bowls. Spread the icing with a knife and make sure that each colour is dry before adding the next.

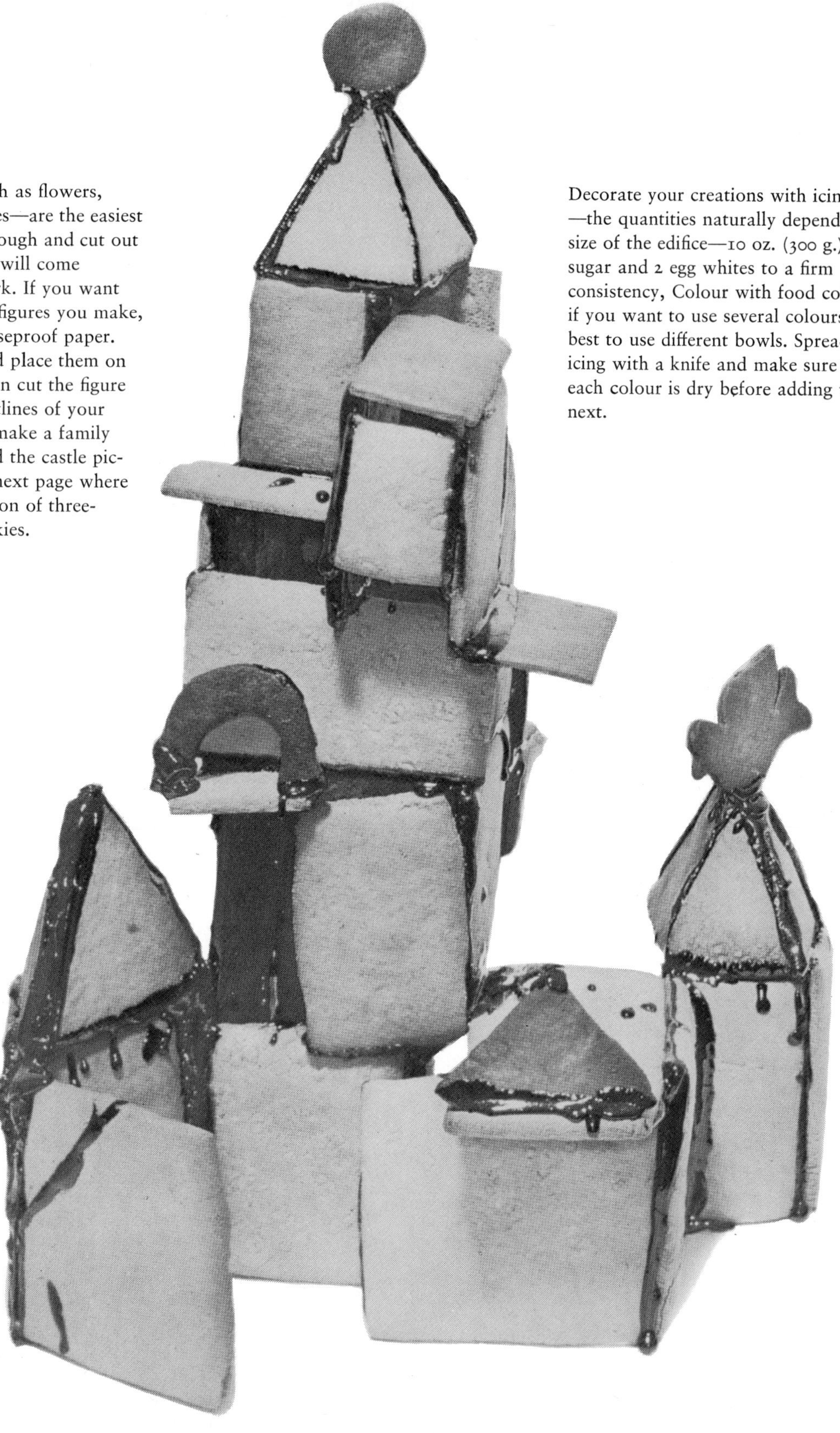

Three-dimensional ginger cookies, like the impressive fairy-tale castle on page 157, and the charming train opposite, are built up of several parts which must later be joined together. Keep an eye on your creations during the baking. Have a look at them half-way through the usual baking time; a section of your train or castle may have melted so much that it has lost its shape. If so, mould it gently back into its original shape with a knife. You can strengthen the sides and corners of your works of art by applying a little melted sugar. Do this very carefully with a knife after you have taken the biscuits out of the oven. Let the sugar harden before icing.

Finally, decorate your work with icing, as described in detail on the previous pages.

Perhaps you—or your family—don't like trains, castles or ginger men. There are dozens of other attractive things you can make with gingerbread.

And if you yourself are not keen on cooking and baking, no one will be any the worse off, because you have probably found in this book enough things in your own line to amuse you—to occupy you creatively. And that was the reason for it all.